UNSOLVED YORKSHIRE MURDERS

MURDERS

From the Leeds, Bradford and Hull areas
STEPHEN WADE

A FOUL DEEDS SPECIAL

Series Editor
Brian Elliott

Wharncliffe Books

First Published in Great Britain in 2004 by
Wharncliffe Local History
an imprint of
Pen and Sword Books Ltd.
47 Church Street
Barnsley
South Yorkshire
S70 2AS
Copyright © Stephen Wade, 2004
ISBN: 1-903425-60-3

Typeset in 11/13pt Plantin by Mac Style Ltd, Scarborough.
Printed and bound in England by
CPI UK.

Pen and Sword Books Ltd incorporates the Imprints of
Pen & Sword Aviation, Pen & Sword Maritime,
Pen & Sword Military, Wharncliffe Local History,
Pen & Sword Select, Pen and Sword Military Classica
and Leo Cooper.

For a complete list of Pen & Sword titles please contact
PEN & SWORD BOOKS LIMITED
47 Church Street
Barnsley
South Yorkshire
S70 2BR
England
E-mail: enquiries@pen-and-sword.co.uk
Website: www.pen-and-sword.co.uk

Contents

Introduction

A quick scan through the archives reveals the sorry tale: a catalogue of lonely deaths, mostly of people lonely and exposed to the dark streets or the risk of spending time with strangers. The headlines look like this:

October 28   1938   *Body of Phyllis Hirst aged 8, found in lane at Horton Green, Bradford.*

September 9   1944   *Body of Harrison* [Harry] *Graham, taxicab owner of Bradford, found in his cab.*

June 12   1953   *Body of Mrs Catherine Mary Odgen* [Kitty Bannon] *found in Bowling Park, Bradford. Sex death.*

These stories and dozens more illustrate how stories with incredibly complex plots and side-effects may be reduced to these minimal statements. The unsolved murder is a conundrum, and the human mind cannot resist the challenge, like sitting down to do *The Times* Crossword again.

But the tales of the unsolved go back a long way. We may begin with a brief mention of an eighteenth century event.

In October 1752, a London newspaper reported a bizarre and perplexing robbery and assault that had taken place in Leeds. A certain Mr Fearn was attacked by a figure he called a 'sham Devil'. The figure had roughly-made horns and took up a 'frightful posture' to attack. He struck in the early hours, first stole a gold watch, and then Mr Fearn reported that he was then severely beaten and feared for his life, yelling 'Murder' as loudly as he could. The poor man grappled with the assailant and was robust enough to try to restrain him, but was attacked all the more savagely. Finally, the 'Devil' ran off.

Fearn didn't quite die, but the mystery remains, and it will surely be unsolved as time goes on. But this has all the elements that attract people to such horrendous events: mystery, shock, the victim against adversity, and a desperate criminal.

We all like an unsolved case: it challenges at the same time as it frustrates. To the media, anything unsolved is going to run on and on, and in some sense, 'stay news'. Regular features in local papers about the anniversary of an unsolved murder certainly help to sell copies, just as much as they might flush out the guilty party. Unsolved also means *unresolved*: that is, not tied up and neatly sorted out, with the satisfying closure of a 'good tale.' Of course, real life crime is of a different nature to invented crime, but even the most heart-rending stories of murder and suffering have a place in the grand narrative of that fascination human beings have with homicide.

The great, well-established scale unsolved non-political murders such as those of The Black Dahlia, Bible John Killings and The Zodiac Killer, all continue to fascinate; but the suburbs and the side-streets, cottages and canals of northern England have their share of unsolved cases, tales of great drama and malevolence. This book is a selection of some of the most intriguing of these murders, mostly in the West Riding and in Hull. There are famous cases slightly further afield, such as the Gorse Hall case of 1909 or the Elsie Frost murder in Wakefield in 1965, or which the suspect was acquitted.

Of course, this book leaves something for the reader to do: the facts are there but not the resolution. These are stories waiting for an ending. Naturally, the more sophisticated DNA testing and application become as the years pass, the more our chances of catching up with some killers from the past increase. But there is still a place for the reader with a curiosity about human behaviour, depravity and extreme violence, to generate some thoughts about these cases.

For instance, on 10 June 1957, a kind old lady who kept a sweet shop in Halifax was bludgeoned to death, and for a small sum of money. She was apparently kept in the back room for some time before she died. It is a case typical of so many unsolved murders: something evil done by casual visitors to a town, rogues passing through a place, desperate people willing to take a chance if offered. Top officers from Scotland Yard came north. Tracker dogs were brought from a crack team at Wakefield. The killer was never traced. But that does not mean that he or she never will be found. The mystery goes on being considered.

Readers of crime love a whodunnit, and they love playing detective; yet somehow when actual killings are considered, there is an intensely human confrontation with some unpalatable facts: children attacked and strangled at night; old and feeble people attacked and left to die just 'for kicks'; householders attacked and slaughtered in their own homes for a few pounds. Something in us wants justice to be done. Hence the fascination with these cases goes on.

There is also, of course, the expectancy always in the minds of both relatives of victims and indeed the law officers who have spent months in an enquiry and finally had to close the books. Now, with DNA becoming increasingly sophisticated, 'unsolved' may not be a word of such finality. For instance, the murder of Susan Long in Norfolk in 1970 is (as I write in 2004) being revisited as forensic scientists have extracted DNA from blood on garments – and the blood group of the killer is a rare one. The original work of taking 3,700 statements may not have been wasted time.

The other level of interest here is in the momentary glimpse of otherwise unknown lives, those shreds of textless history led by unremarkable people going about their routine. In fact, these tales show how that routine may be an enemy. Routine opens up something of the individual and their habits, and so makes them open, visible, assailable and potentially a victim.

The research behind these stories has involved travelling to the places involved, trawling through old newspapers, and interpreting information from those aspects of local history that play a part in understanding the history of crime within known communities. In seeing these tasks through, I have appreciated the previous writing done by A A Clarke, Paul Langan, Andy Owens, Matthew Spicer and Louise Pearce.

I would also like to thank my editor, Brian Elliott, staff at the *Evening Courier,* the librarians at Leeds City Libraries, and Stephen Carter of the *Huddersfield Examiner* for their help.

Special thanks are due to Jayne Marsden at the *Yorkshire Post,* Marie Campbell, whose book *Curious Tales of Old West Yorkshire* was fascinatingly helpful, and to Issy Shannon, publisher of *Milltown Memories*. Issy has given invaluable help in providing images from her archive.

I must also thank the people on the streets who gave me stories: ordinary people who had merely snippets of information, but which helped to make up the full story.

Line drawings are by Laura Carter, who has done a wonderful job in bringing alive some of the sad and desperate faces from these stories.

Part I

Borderline and Bizarre Unsolved

Cases on the fringe of the unsolved category

There are some cases that illustrate the profound interest we have in unsolved mysteries. The example of a disappearance is the most significant one, and there are several of these in the fairly recent history of Yorkshire. As these are likely but not definitely murder cases, I left them out of the main stories, but a short survey of the most baffling of these follows here.

Robin Hood, 1347
Why not start with a Yorkshire story somewhere in that misty land of imagination somewhere between history and myth?

Robin Hood's Grave. Laura Carter

This is the case of Robin Hood. Historians are clear that his grave lies at Hartshead, near Brighouse, beneath tangled undergrowth, neglected and forlorn. Here is a case of an unsolved mystery back in 1347, according to some sources. The mystery lies in whether or not he was slain by the prioress of Kirklees Priory, whether she was actually there at the time, and why she would want him dead.

In the popular literature about Robin, the story goes that the prioress, Elizabeth de Staynton, bled him as a treatment when he arrived at her home, apparently dying. With her lover, Red Roger of Doncaster, she is supposed to have killed him in this way. In true legendary folk narrative tradition, Robin says he is to be buried on the spot where his last fired arrow falls. This was 600 yards from the gatehouse.

Last year, (2003), the *Most Haunted* television team of investigators went there for a programme, and did much to perpetuate the myth, drawing attention to the rusty old iron railing above the grave and retelling the prioress story. But who was she and did she kill him? The writer, Barbara Green, has convincingly shown that, if the date of death is actually 1347, not 1247 as on the tomb, then the prioress at the time was Mary Startin, not Elizabeth de Staynton. History says she died of the plague, and literature says she may have killed herself in remorse for killing Robin.

As Barbara points out, we need a motive, and the only one suggested is that Robin opposed ecclesiastical corruption, as graphically described by Chaucer in his *Pardoner's Tale* (written probably around fifty years after this date). We have to say that it was a nasty and slow method of killing if indeed it was so, and there is plenty of mystery in the bare facts, without recourse to theories of sacrifice or even vampirism.

The story is a useful one to begin a collection like this: a mix of conjecture, narrative and some painstaking scholarship on the part of writers like Barbara Green. Her researches have led anyone interested in the history of 'open cases' to place Robin firmly in Yorkshire, rather than in Nottinghamshire history. We need to be reminded that Sherwood Forest at that time extended all the way up to West Yorkshire.

The Body at Pecket Well, 1850

Some stories are gruesome and savage, but offer us a story that will probably always remain an enigma. They are often horrendous deaths occurring in desolate places and outside any documented community history. When these tales are told, they offer barbaric acts and bloody deeds. Such a case is that of the corpse found on Shackleton Moor in 1830, above Pecket Well.

The body in question was discovered in a sack by Thomas Greenwood. The sack clearly meant that someone put it there, and that someone was most likely the killer. In a story deserving of the most atmospheric yarns of Thomas Hardy, we learn that the body was carried to the Robin Hood Inn at Pecket Well, to be displayed, with the hope that someone in the vicinity might recognise the person. So there it lay, tanned like the peat-bog men found in Jutland or Cheshire, with the red whiskers in the light of the room, and the hard, weathered limbs out for all to see as they enjoyed a pint.

Naturally, crowds came to stare at the curiosity, and the landlord, Thomas Whiteley, was indeed very pleased at this development. The inevitable happened, and body-parts were

Pecket Well. Longstaff collection

stolen as macabre souvenirs. A local man, Launcelot Feather, even purloined two of the cadaver's teeth, wrapping them in paper and walking off with some delight.

Eventually, the poor man was identified: he was named by his mother and sister as being one Thomas Townsend of Stairs Hole Farm, Oxenhope. He had been missing for twenty-eight years. What made the identification pretty certain was that the women saw the club foot, and also noted that a knee-cap was missing. This had been as a result of a domestic accident, and the family had kept the knee-cap at home, all those years.

Historian Issy Shannon comments that a man later did make a confession to the murder, and said that it happened after a quarrel. But no inquest was ever held on the body in the bog on those wild moors.

Poisoning in Keighley? 1854

John Sagar, master of Exley Head workhouse at Oakworth near Howarth, walked out of the Spring Assizes at Leeds in 1858 a free man. Yet many thought him the poisoner of his wife. Conflicting medical evidence about her death was the basic reason for him being free. There was plenty of doubt

Howarth in the 1850s. Laura Carter, from E G Gaskell's original

about the circumstances and causes of Barbara Sagar's death – and there is still to this day.

Barbara had lost nine children before she herself fell ill, and she died at the age of thirty nine, after a long and painful period of illness. Arsenic poison was the apparent cause, and her husband had been dispensing this to her. The couple were jointly responsible for running the workhouse, and the place had been searched after rumours about Sagar's guilt were circulated. After all, there had been far more child – deaths than the average in his family – even in those times of high infant mortality rates.

Moreover, the couple's life and morality were questionable, and there was a very unwholesome side to their habits. Young girls were procured for their marriage bed, and John was apparently a man with a brutal element in him; he was said to beat his wife, and it was said that he was 'low' and 'despicable.' Prostitution was rife in the area, and the couple's sexual habits were perhaps not that rare in this specific community.

What is recorded, however, is that Barbara confided that she thought she was being poisoned. When it came to the post-mortem, though, the uncertainties arrive. Dr John Mulligan was the official doctor for the workhouse, and he clearly might be biased in his opinion; it was therefore no surprise when he stated that the woman's death gave no reason to suspect foul play. The next doctor to investigate, Dr Morley of Leeds, thought differently: he found a large amount of arsenic in the deceased.

The case highlights something that must have been reasonably common in the social fabric of West Yorkshire at this time: there are a number of examples on record of death by the inaccurate administering of drugs. In fact, poisoning was something of an epidemic of crime in the 1840s and later. There were efforts to streamline the dispensing of the substance. It must also be recalled that there had been the case of Rebecca Smith, who poisoned eight children for the given reason that they might 'come to want.' In the 1860s, the most common victims of the 'white powder' were children under five.

People were habitual users of several highly dangerous medicines at that time. This is a perfect example of those possibly unsolved murder cases that actually generate parallel stories, and Marie Campbell has pointed out that Mulligan was a Freemason, along with Sagar, and that would cloud the waters of objectivity in the intercourse of the trial and investigation. Yet more intriguing in the tale of this couple's life is their social decline. Hartley points out that they sold all the contents of their smart property in Cullingworth, six years before Barbara's death.

This coda is truly a stunning paradox: leaving such opulence and selling all their real wealth suggests that something drastic was happening. He was a painter and glazier, and not as far as we know in any trouble. But surely there is an unexplained factor here – maybe something that had to be hidden, or a need to be elsewhere – and quickly? One suspects that there is a moral rather than simply a financial reason behind Sagar's decline.

Suspicious Death at the *Dog and Partridge*, 1889

William Clarke, a stone mason of Heptonstall, clearly enjoyed a drink, and he liked the company of the local lasses. A particularly long and intense binge, and some serious partying, led to his death on 8 August 1889, and the case is unsolved and full of questions to this day.

Hepstonstall is indeed a high fastness in a wild part of Calderdale, high above the Lancashire road. Cars need first gear to carry on up the loftier, narrower lanes which eventually lead onto the barren moors of Oxenhope and then Howarth. It is also a place associated with the eighteenth century coiner gangs, an outfit quite capable of murder too, if threatened. So Clarke's case is one of many in a tough, violent place.

William, brother Thomas and a whole gaggle of young women enjoyed a drinking session in the pub through the afternoon that summer day. When Thomas left, William retired upstairs with the female company and had a good time. It was in the early evening that William was left alone to sleep off some of the effects of the drink, but he was seen downstairs

Townsgate, Heptonstall. Longstaff Collection

later, eating veal pie and taking some whisky. After that, people had seen him sitting alone, late in the evening.

But then, not long before midnight, William was found in the street, mortally wounded. He lasted just a few hours, and died as a result of these severe injuries, in the early hours of the next day.

Evidence given later by brother Thomas suggests some physical attack and theft. William had reported that he had sensed someone going through the pockets of his coat as he was sleepy and not really aware of things. He also told his brother that he had received a blow, being 'knocked gormless' by some unknown attacker.

At this point, everything becomes clouded in mystery, half-truth and rumour. For instance, a woman living nearby reports that she heard loud groans from the street, walked out to investigate, and heard the dying man say something about Sally, apparently referring to Sally having harmed him in some way: 'Sally, thou shouldn't 'a done that!'

But common sense pointed to a more rational explanation – that William in his drunken state had fallen as he tried to work his way out of the attic window, perhaps mistaking it for an exit door. But if he had done so, he would have almost certainly been seen by the innkeeper's family as he walked through their main bedroom. In doing that walk, he would have had to climb a shaky staircase and cross a wooden attic floor wearing his heavy boots, then go through the window to his death, without being seen or heard. There were, however, marks on the window sill and it looks as though his injuries could have been consistent with such a fall.

In spite of all this police thinking, the mood around town was hostile and unpredictable. The open verdict returned did little to appease the large crowd assembled in Bridge Lane, and the people booed the officers as they walked in Hope Street. Some witnesses even had to be given police protection. The local journalists at the time, obviously nosing around and talking to people who never came forward to the law, or who were never sought out by the investigators, were suspicious, and agreed that there had been an attack leading to death. What stirred up this kind of thought was a detail such as the fact that his watch was missing – and indeed it was handed in later, by a local girl called 'Sally a'the Dog' who said that she had been trusted with looking after it on that drunken night.

Was this a murder? It seems highly likely. Clarke's drunkenness was 'public' and so he would be perceived as vulnerable and an easy target for some around the community at the time. He would have been an easy target. It was a lawless time and a tough place. Money was hard to come by, and William had plenty to spend that night.

Father Borynski, 1953

On 13 July 1953, a Polish priest, Father Henrik Borynski, after taking a phone call, merely said, 'All right, I go ...' and his housekeeper watched him walk away, never to be seen or heard of again. Some writers refer to this as a 'murder case' but there was no body and there were no real suspects, despite the suspiciously questionable data about 'Communist agents' around at the time. A seeming attack on another priest, Father Martynellis, who was leader of the Lithuanian community in Bradford, followed. But there are too many suppositions and urban tales here. The main line is that Martynellis was found with 'Be silent, priest' written by matchsticks next to him.

Borynski's landlady, Irena Beck, called the police. After that, there must have been some thinking going on relating to higher politics, as the CID and MI5 were called in to investigate. Certainly, as Frank Fraser has written (he was around there at the time), there was a great deal of anti-Communist feeling. Borynski had been criticising these people from his pulpit.

The priest had left with only a few pounds in his pocket and yet a large amount of money was in his bank account. He even left his wallet and other important papers and possessions behind him when he left the lodgings in Little Horton Lane that day. He was chaplain to a large community: around 1,500 people. So he was an important figure. But was he important enough to be grabbed in the streets by the secret police or agents from the Eastern Block?

One line of thought, from no less a police officer than Bob Taylor, suspects that it is

Father Borynski. Laura Carter

impossible to believe that Martynellis was not involved in the disappearance in some way. He believes that the hierarchy of the Catholic Church at the time knew more than they actually stated at the time of the investigation. One thing is sure when one looks at the political climate at the time: feelings ran high with regard to the Communists. Just a few years before, a rally in Huddersfield, with a large turn-out of Yorkshire Poles, had speakers who made it clear that the vast numbers of Poles then prisoners in Russian camps was not tolerable. There were demonstrations when Kruschev visited Britain in 1956.

It is easy to jump to conclusions without evidence, but the tantalising final words of Borynski do suggest that he had an appointment, and that he did not expect that meeting or chore to be his final one.

Disappearing Coalman, 1961

1961 must have been a tough and frustrating year for the detectives of Humberside police. First a quiet man inexplicably disappeared, his coal lorry being found abandoned in Hull city centre, and then a man called Richardson, who had been a lodger with Fred Wilkinson, also went missing. Surely there was a connection, and surely Richardson was the prime suspect? But it was much more difficult than that, sorting out the mess.

Sightings of Richardson came in from all directions; first he was seen in the area where the van was left, and then he was spotted in pubs around the Paull area of Hull. He had reportedly been sighted sleeping out rough in the country, and also in Beverley. It took ages before anything developed, but finally, he was found and arrested in Rosedale Grove, well out of the centre beyond the Ferensway junction with Spring Bank.

Frederick Wilson. Laura Carter

Albion Street, Hull, where Wilson's lorry was left. The author

An element of farce creeps in when we learn that Richardson was severely injured in custody, slipping and then being taken to hospital. The local people waited expectantly for the announcement of the killer found, and of course, some knowledge of where Fred Wilkinson might be. Was he even dead? All that transpired was that Richardson appeared at the Magistrates' Court and was given a short sentence for non-payment of fines. So nothing was resolved.

What happened to Fred Wilkinson remains a mystery. As A A Clarke points out, Fred was a strong, robust man, used to lifting bags of coal, and had been as sturdy as ever in spite of having a heart problem a few years before the disappearance. The root of the mystery may lie in the fact that Bernard

Richardson, while lodging at the Wilkinsons' house, had a liaison with Fred's daughter, and Bernard was a married man.

But the guesswork goes on, with Fred's disappearance never being explained.

Mystery and Myth off Holderness Road, 1963

Another disappearance in Hull concerns a fifteen-year-old boy, Frederick Dean, and the word around at the time was that Dean's name had been in some of the diaries of the Moors murderers. Their trial was going on in Chester at the time, and the daily papers insisted on spinning amazingly bizarre urban

Franklin Street, Hull, home of Fred Dean. The author

myths about the pair of killers, but to reach Hull was an amazing thought at the time. What it does suggest, though, is the public outrage and bafflement at the disappearance of a teenager.

Frederick was fifteen, and had been living at 43, Franklin Street; he was noticeable as he had a definite limp and dragged one leg as he walked. As with so many young murder victims, his case entails a simple, everyday walk out along the street, and into oblivion. He was merely going to visit his grandparents. No trace of him was ever found.

The usual steps were taken: a neighbourhood search led by Frederick's father (who at one point collapsed), and then further afield, even as far as the estuary. Time went on and ordinary people maintained the search; the Head of the police division, Superintendent Ron Joyce, released and circulated a full description.

The emotional centre of this tragedy is that the boy was taking a Christmas present to his grandmother – and never arrived there. The case typifies that version of unsolved cases which results from a chance encounter, an opportunist crime.

East Pool, towards Holderness. Three unsolved cases occurred in streets off this road. The author

Lamentably, this one had dire consequences for the whole neighbourhood. They must have felt peculiarly exposed and in need of more vigilance.

A UFO killing? 1980

Tingley, in the heart of the Leeds-Bradford conurbation, is a long way from the Pennine town of Todmorden, but this story concerns one Zigmund Adamski, who walked out into a Tingley street, only to be found, dead, on a coal heap in Todmorden five days later. Although the coroner pronounced death by natural causes, the body had mysterious burn marks, oval-shaped, on the head and neck.

It has to be said that, according to Andy Owens, there were several UFO sightings over the Calder Valley at that time. Zigmund was found on top of the coal, with no signs of the heap being disturbed. He was weak and ill, and could not have climbed up the coal so easily. Was there an 'alien' story here?

Many police officers that night reported UFOs; one of them even underwent hypnotic regression. Just as these moves failed to be conclusive, so did the forensic studies. The only thing we know for sure is that the victim died of fright. The dead face showed an expression of stark horror.

Zigmund had no enemies as far as we know. But there are teasing questions, such as whether he was kidnapped. As Andy Owens points out, nothing so far satisfactorily explains how a sick man was found twenty miles from home, shirtless, covered in burns, and on top of a coal pile with a face showing absolute terror. A Halifax pathologist, Dr Alan Edwards, had stated that there were no injuries to explain the cause of death. The search for the facts goes on, and all we can say, a little ironically, is 'the truth is out

Zygmund Adamski. Laura Carter

Todmorden, the town centre today. The author

there.' From time to time, the history of violent crime raises questions about the varieties of murder: the causes, the means of expression, and most intriguing of all, the relation between a person's chosen lifestyle and a strikingly remarkable version of death that person undergoes. When, as in this case, that death is truly enigmatic, the normal parameters of detective and police thinking tend to find their limits.

The Bakery Victim, 1977

There are other kinds of mystery cases in which the tragedy of an innocent man going 'down' takes centre stage. This is such a story: that of the murder of Carole Wilkinson in Thornbury, Bradford, in 1977. She was attacked from behind on Woodhall Road, battered to death with a 50 pound stone. A savage sexual attack followed this. There were no immediate suspects, and time went on.

But then someone related to gardener Anthony Steel came forward with the information that a keyring in Steel's possession had belonged to the dead girl. Steel denied being anywhere near the murder scene, and had references to time spent with workmates. But he was questioned at length, for a period of almost eight hours. Under pressure, after the fourth interview, he confessed. At the trial, the accused's lawyers said they had had a telephone confession, but the case for prosecution pressed on relentlessly.

Steel was sentenced to life for murder, and as Louise Pearce notes, 'the police were happy to have found her killer'. Incredibly, twenty years passed before the television programme, Rough Justice, demonstrated his innocence. He had gone through the agony of a long spell in prison, and as an innocent man. He has been cleared. Now we have an instance of a case being re-opened. Amazingly, at the time of the sentence, and after the admission under stress, it was known by some parties in the affair that Steel had a specific mental handicap. Michael Mansfield QC is reported by Louise Pearce as saying that Steel had been 'badgered' into confession and that all related statements had been made only in general terms.

Eugene Aram: The Mystery Continues, 1759

There are many more famous cases which are predominantly agreed to be stories with a closure and a certain degree of satisfaction in the end of a tortuous narrative of victims and aggressors. Many of these are very widely known, and do not need retelling here, but there is one celebrated eighteenth century case that demonstrates how the fascination with open-ended stories and tales of crime unpunished goes on: that of the schoolmaster of Knaresborough, Eugene Aram. Perhaps this case shows the classic example of a felon turning King's Evidence, when Henry Terry did so and officers went down to Lynn to arrest Aram while he was teaching.

Eugene Aram. From an old engraving (1903)

But, as Peter Walker says, 'Even today, questions are asked about the guilt of Eugene Aram as scholars attempt to decide whether or not he should have been convicted of murder.' Aram taught in Knaresborough and also in the South of England, but his criminal activities were initially merely fraud, as he worked alongside two other men. Essentially, what had incriminated Aram was his involvement in a scam to raise money, linked with one Daniel Clark, and after Aram had left the town to go south and work in Lynn, the body of Clark was found.

Clark had disappeared about the time that Aram had left for Lynn, and now, after the passage of time, clothing was found buried in Aram's garden. After a long and complicated series of events, Houseman, another associate of Aram, led the law to another corpse and insisted that this one was Clark's, and that Aram had killed him.

Aram spoke in his own defence at York Assizes, and the case was crying out for some kind of basic forensic knowledge. But instead, Aram was left alone, with what we might now call a fit-up against him, as thieves had fallen out. He was doomed, and it is ironical that Aram's story, essentially that of the remorseful intellectual who mixed with the wrong sort of person, has gone down in literature, as he was the subject of works by Thomas Hood and Bulwer-Lytton.

What it shows an historian of crime is that in any consorting group of miscreants, victims are often picked out by the less morally troubled members, and when the flak flies,

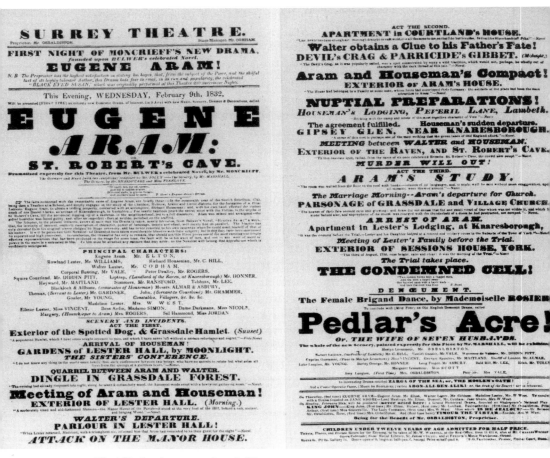

Playbill of a drama on Aram's life. From an old illustration (1903)

the victim is singled out and others run for safety. Aram's story presents us with a template for those kinds of mysterious cases in which, the law at the time lacking sophisticated forensic knowledge, history has left an open box, and we have to sift through the contents hoping for a discovery.

Knaresborough has more than its share of murder connections: one of the men who killed Thomas a Becket, Hugh de Morville, was from the town; Richard II was imprisoned here before being taken to Pontefract to meet a violent end in 1399. But the tale of Eugene Aram will always be the most celebrated and puzzling. We are not even sure, to this day, what the exact medical evidence was regarding the body of Clark, the victim; nor do we know for certain whether a mysterious fourth man involved framed Aram for the deed. Nor are we sure that Aram did not kill three men.

Part II

Around Bradford, Wharfedale and Calderdale

CHAPTER ONE

The Coiners' Gang Murder
1771

Around Calderdale, the story of the Coiners of Heptonstall and the ultimate capture and execution of David Hartley, provides one of the most dramatic episodes in the history of crime and disorder in the area. The events leading up to the murder of the exciseman William Deighton are truly stranger than the most tense thriller in

Towngate, Heptonstall, showing the Cross Inn. Longstaff Collection

fiction. Deighton had been hot on their trail, hounding the gang for clipping the coins of the realm, melting down the excess metal and then coining more currency. He was within a few days of having them in hand, when he was murdered on Swires Road in Halifax, near his home.

The atmosphere around the valleys of Calderdale at the time was one of recrimination and suspicion. Any one of a number of men could have been implicated and their fate would have been the noose at York Castle. Although members and those on the fringe of the gang were living in quiet places strung out across the area, they would, naturally, consort and drink together. One such meeting, at the Cross Inn, Heptonstall, became the scene of a murder which has to go down in the annals of homicide in England as one of the most unbelievably savage and cruel one could ever imagine.

Only a few months before these men gathered at the inn, Hartley had been executed, and his body lay in the nearby churchyard. Feelings were running high. It was a question of *who might be next to the gallows?* In this atmosphere, a farm labourer called Abraham Ingham was known to be one of Deighton's informers, and he had received the handsome sum of £100 blood money for his exertions. He would have to be taken care of: his mouth shut forever. On this particular night, he was in a crowd of what seemed to be a gathering of reasonably affable fellow-drinkers in this lofty spot up the slopes of the town. But Ingham did the worst thing he could possibly have done at that time – brag about knowing the other men involved in the Deighton murder. He also declared his intention to give their names to the authorities.

What a fatal error of judgement that was. The loosening of his tongue with alcohol was his death warrant. But the manner of his death was horrific in the extreme. The men grabbed him and forced him to the large open fireplace. There was no way he could escape their grasp, as he saw them heat some tongs, and then ruthlessly fasten these around his neck. His head was then thrust into the flames. The gang members were yet more determined to see him suffer and die in agony. They dropped burning coals down his trousers. One account actually states that the poor man was spread-eagled over the fire and roasted to death.

Ingham died a violent and terrible death. Yet this is an unsolved murder – simply because the men charged were acquitted through lack of evidence. One has to say that any witnesses to this horrible killing would have been strongly persuaded to remain silent and keep well away from any officers of the law. Astoundingly, one of the gang was said to be a woman. The milk of human kindness was absent that night up in the steep lanes of Heptonstall.

CHAPTER TWO

The Moorcock Inn Killing
1832

In 1959, the newly-formed Saddleworth History Club gathered to pit their wits against the riddle of perhaps the most gripping and dramatic unsolved murder case in the history of Yorkshire. They could come to no firm conclusions, after running through the known facts about six possible suspects who may or may not have been responsible for a bloody double murder long ago, in 1832, on the barren moors at Uppermill.

The victims were 84 year-old landlord of the Moorcock Inn, William Bradbury, and his massively strong son, Thomas, 46. Their bodies had been discovered by Bill's pretty grand-daughter, Mary, as she came to find out why Uncle Tom had

The Moorcock Inn (now demolished) as it was in c.1900. Laura Carter

not taken her out to see some strolling players earlier that
night.

The story has everything the reader would ask of a murder
story on the wild moors: an old man, William, called Bill
O'Jacks as he had inherited the inn from his father, Jack; the
tall and sturdy son, Tom, the pretty young woman who had
been promised her grandfather's wealth, and a bunch of ne'er-
do-wells around the place, also called Bradbury, who have
always been top suspects.

Bill was too fond of talking about his distrust of banks and
bragging about his stash of ready money which was concealed
somewhere in the vicinity. It is recorded that some of the
regulars listened intently to all this, and tried to find out where
the money was. But who would argue with the Bradbury men?
Tom was huge, and was in the habit of grabbing anybody who
made a nuisance of themselves, and throwing them over the
back wall.

But the Red Bradbury clan, always making trouble and
brooding around the place, overstepped the mark one day and
were found poaching on Bill's land. Tom took hold of one and
the process of law started, the crucial fact being that Tom was
to have been the main witness when the case came up at
Pontefract the day after the murder.

The murder scene was horrendous. Poor Mary had walked
in upon a nightmarish scene of gore and destruction. The
rooms and furniture were trashed. There was evidence that
there had been a titanic struggle as the big man had fought for
his life, most likely against many assailants. Tom had been
brutally attacked, his face covered in gashes; old Bill, however,
was not quite dead, and managed to say something sounding
like 'Pat.' In that brief grunted utterance lies the foundation of
the mystery and the doubts about the range of suspects.

As there were several potential interpretations of the word
'pat', the confusion and speculations arose in rapid succession.
There were Irish labourers working nearby on the roads and
they were of course referred to as *pats* or *paddies*. But there
were pedlars close too, and they were called the Burn Platters,
so pat/plat was a possibility. To make matters worse, one of the
men who had clearly shown an interest in the location of the

hidden cash was called Reuben Platt. What could be more puzzling for any investigator than this plethora of syllables all so similar?

A central piece of information in the enquiry is the fact that one of the indicted poachers said, openly, that Tom Bradbury would not be appearing at Pontefract. He had boasted this while walking through Meltham. How could he know this, unless he was directly involved? But when the time of the attack was established, it seemed impossible that anyone from the Platt dwelling could have covered the ground and returned in the given timescale. However, the line of thought that poachers tend to know the terrain they inhabit so well that they would know short-cuts obviously arose and has been considered.

Until the time that the Moorcock was pulled down, in 1937, the murder and the surrounding area had been the subject of morbid tourism and of local folklore, with ghost stories attached to the tale as well. The best guide to this impact is perhaps in the words on the tombstone of the victims in Saddleworth churchyard:

Those who now talk of far-famed Greenfield's hills,
will think of Bill o' Jack's and Tom o'Bills,
such interest did their tragic end excite,
that ere they were removed from human sight,
thousands on thousands daily came to see
the bloody scene of the catastrophe.

CHAPTER THREE

The Toll-House Murder
1850

To a modern detective or forensic scientist, the scene in front of Constable Dugdale as he walked into the Hebden Bridge toll house on 28 September 1850 would have been a professional disaster. The locals had stepped in, cleaned up, whitewashed the walls, washed the corpse and generally scattered around a number of misleading 'clues' to further confound an already puzzling case.

The dead man was James Smith, keeper of the toll-house, and also something of a small salesman, as he also sold refreshments to the general populace. He was found with his throat cut. When first people came on the crime scene, there was blood on the walls, furniture was turned over and curtains were torn. Smith was lying on the bed when the police arrived, washed and laid out! From the moment that a young boy had found the body and screamed out around the village that 'Jammy's dead!' the locals had moved into action.

None of this helped matters at all. Constable Dugdale soon realised that this was hardly a suicide, as was first thought. The pillow showed the imprint of two heads recently occupying the bed; then an amateur detective, a Reverend Rhodes, arrived and muddied the water by suggesting that, as the bed had not been made for some time, Smith may have slept on alternate sides. This confusion was to mar the whole investigation. As the suspects were brought in, things were to become even more perplexing. But the fact was that such extreme wounds could not have been self-inflicted. It was a murder case.

First in line was the dead man's known enemy, a tailor from Burnley called Enoch Helliwell. They had recently fallen out, as the tailor owed money for toll fees, and Smith was prosecuting him. He was known to harbour thoughts of revenge and retribution towards the toll-house keeper.

e Hebden-Bridge
MURDER.
£100 REWARD.

Some Person or Persons having on the 28th of September, 1850, feloniously killed and murdered JAMES SMITH, of King-Street, near Hebden-Bridge, Toll Collector, by cutting his Throat. A REWARD of £100 will be paid by Her Majesty's Government, to any Person who shall give such Information and Evidence as shall lead to the discovery and conviction of the Murderer, or Murderers.

And SIR GEORGE GREY, Bart., Secretary of State, will advise the Grant of Her Majesty's Gracious

PARDON

to any Accomplice, not being the Person who actually commi--ed the Murder, who shall give such Information and Evidence as shall lead to the same results.

Information to be given to the CONSTABLES of STANSFIELD, or to MR. HEAP, Sergeant of Police, or to

A. GREENWOOD EASTWOOD,
8th October, 1850.   *SOLICITOR, TODMORDEN.*

Walton, Printer, Todmorden.

Reward poster, 1850. Longstaff Collection

The Old Bar-House. Longstaff Collection

Smith had not been killed for money: £3 of toll money was still in place, and other cash was found, to a total of £15 – a considerable sum then. Robbery was clearly not the motive in this case. So Helliwell was in the frame. But the man had a sound alibi. Lots of his Burnley friends testified that he was with them that night. Also, a certain John Spencer had written to Helliwell, telling him that Smith was dead and that 'you will not meet your opponent at the Leeds Quarter Sessions... he was found this morning with his throat cut.'

Now enter the other main suspect, a young mother's boy called William Green, who had been the last man seen with Smith on that evening. At first, Green said he was guilty, and blood-stained clothes had been found in his home. It seemed to be all sorted out. But then Green retracted and talked about seeing a stranger at the toll house that night. A full enquiry followed, at the Cross Inn, and witnesses said they had seen Green with Smith that night, but their description of the clothing he wore did not tally with the stained clothes they found at the young man's home. One John Shaw, who had rushed to the toll-house on the cry of murder, had checked the cash box, and then seen Green nearby, but insisted that Green was wearing a check jacket. The stained coat was striped.

Some of the stains were found to be tobacco, but some were indeed blood. The coroner allowed Green to go, but the general suspicions were there and the mood was grim and threatening around the town. At this point, a clasp-knife, clearly the murder weapon, was found not far away, and it was in a place where Green had said he had seen the mystery figure of the stranger change clothing.

The tide turned again, and it was realised that Helliwell, with the obvious motive, could have hired killers to do the deed. He was re-arrested and bailed for £1000, just before the murder weapon was found, and Green was now in the dock. Before the magistrates, it was said that Green was there only on circumstantial evidence, and that the first confession was done under pressure and in conditions of mental turmoil. The 'timid young man who suffered bad dreams', Green, punched his forehead in a demonstrative effort to recall who the man was he had seen that night – but to no avail. Green was released.

The coda to the story concerns a letter written to the police by a Mr Adkinson of Burnley, telling them that Helliwell was indeed the killer. Under arrest again, poor Helliwell had to endure the shame of his public arraignment – one that turned out to be founded on the ravings of a madman. Adkinson was mentally unstable and had no evidence, nor talked any sense, when he was finally brought over the Pennines to make a statement.

What do we know, then, about this dramatic and puzzling case? We know that the blood stains on Green's clothes were never explained. If it was a suicide, it was incredibly violent, a real blood-bath which suggested a prolonged struggle rather than a desire to end it all. We also know that the astonishingly convoluted stories of the suspects were unable to be unknotted at that time, and the lack of forensics obviously never opened up any real police procedure. Green seems to have been quite feeble, weak and dreamy. His demeanour aroused the pity of the magistrates, in spite of a brooding population of villagers who thought him guilty. The truth is out there.

CHAPTER FOUR

The *David Copperfield* Mystery 1866

I n Dickens's novel, *David Copperfield* (1849) the cad, Steerforth, is washed up drowned on a beach at the end of chapter 55, and the narrator comments, '... among the ruins of the home he had wronged I saw him lying with his head upon his arm, as I had often seen him lie at school.' In some murders and mysterious deaths, people end their life on earth in a bizarre mirror-image of events in novels. The tale of the Bradford schoolmaster, Mr Blum, suggests this may well be the case.

In 1866, the *Keighley News* reported on Blum's disappearance. He was second master at Bradford High School, and had last been seen walking towards the railway station on Saturday 28 April. Although a gentleman of 'regular' and 'correct' habits, he had apparently disappeared without trace, and when last seen, he had been carrying no luggage.

Israel Blum had left school at noon and called at a bookseller's in Kirkgate, Byles's shop, to collect the second volume of the Dickens novel he had ordered. He told a colleague that he intended to do some experiments later, but would read a paper at the station first. A train left for Liverpool early that afternoon. He was never seen again in Bradford. The next time he was seen was when his body was found on the beach at Hoylake by two young women.

The stance of the body when found is interesting. A fisherman brought police and a doctor and it was reported that the position was that he was lying in the hollow of a rock, with one hand bent back close to the body, and the throat cut twice. His coat was nearby and later his copy of Dickens was found at Redstones, with a page folded over.

The verdict at the inquest was suicide, but some medical opinion was that there had been foul play. A Dr Dodd had

David Copperfield, frontispiece (from a late Victorian edition, 1890)

looked at the body and was of this opinion. It was a Leeds police officer who told the Head of the Bradford High School to come and verify the identity of the dead man. Colleagues travelled to Birkenhead to perform the unpleasant task of verifying the identity of the corpse. With many more facts assembled by people who knew Blum, it became increasingly likely that he could have been killed.

Possessions were missing from the body, such as a gold chain, and his wallet and spectacles. It was disturbing to think that he had rushed to Liverpool, with very little money on him, and then met with this violent end. No weapons linking the death to suicide were found, and no reason for such an action known to anyone who knew the man. There is only one brief and intriguing clue as to his situation and reasons for leaving Bradford on that day, and this is in a letter to his fiancee who lived in London. In the letter he says that he had a strange letter from a stranger in Leeds. 'He

The Death of Steerforth, a drawing from the 1890 edition.

comes from Hamburg and wishes to see me.... A strange thing is it not?'

What causes more complexity here and calls on the expertise of a Sherlock Holmes, is that we know Blum had a brother, a veteran of the American Civil War, and that the two brothers had met in Bradford a year earlier, and walked to the station together. The brother had apparently been given money from Israel? to enable him to start a fresh life in Australia.   1866 ?

Blum had been seen alive by several people in the early afternoon of the day he died, at Redstones, wearing a hat and spectacles. Here the Dickens connection enters with some mystery. Further medical evidence had pointed out that the body had been virtually bloodless, and had probably been carried from the place of death to the coast. No trace of the possessions ever came to light. Sir George Grey ordered a second inquest. All this achieved was to deepen the puzzle and to ask more difficult questions. But the fact remains that the man eventually buried in Hoylake church had taken a special interest in the Dickens story, and in a rather creepy way, his death echoed the death of the villain Steerforth in Dickens' novel.

The parallels between the death and the fictional death are mainly that there is a new schoolmaster at the school Copperfield attends; Steerforth, former schoolmate and hero, is drowned and washed up after seducing a pure young woman. Steerforth's mother is wealthy and lives in London, like Blum's. Finally, Copperfield's best friends emigrate, just as Blum's brother is meant to do. But the position of Blum's body, if carried to the shore from the killing place by the killer, was placed in a similar position to that of the drowned Steerforth. Why? The obvious but eerie and deviant answer is that a deadly game had been played, and perhaps it was a suicide deal or even a contract killing. The brother had the motive of cash. But more likely is some theory involving an intellectual game, much as more recent pacts have involved works of art and literature.

There is very little left to help any new investigation. Attempts have been made; Marie Campbell had followed leads in the Home Office and in the life of Sir George himself. If it was murder, then the gain was small; if it were a suicide pact, then there are facts about the personal life of Israel Blum that went to the grave with him. If he were some kind of Steerforth figure, then both killer and victim, sharing the textual knowledge, would have seen the death as just, as it was placed in the plot by Dickens – the rewards of malpractice balancing the rewards of virtue. At the heart of the story is a tale of seduction, elopement and corruption in a world with an insistence on the ongoing innocence of simple folk like the Peggotty family and David himself, with his Dora. Some twisted mind may have transmuted fiction into reality and put murder into the plot – for real. Who knows, Blum may even have been to watch Dickens read his work: the great man was in Bradford in 1855 just after Christmas, to perform readings from *A Christmas Carol* at St George's Hall. Whatever the link was between the nature of Dickens' book and this lonely death, it remains unknown.

CHAPTER FIVE

A Northern Ripper Killing?
Bradford 1888

The disappearance of yet another child from the streets of a northern industrial city would not normally cause a stir for the historian of crime. But the case of the mutilation and murder of little John Gill, of 41, Thorncliffe Road, is something rather different, if we are to believe the speculations of Patricia Cornwell. In her book, *Portrait of a Killer* (2002), she examines this child-murder and notes not only parallels with the Whitechapel murders of the Ripper, but also some slight evidence that the Ripper was in fact the painter, Walter Sickert.

The latter fact may be easily disputed, but the actual nature of the killing of Gill does bear remarkable similarities to the London murders. The only problem tends to be that, in spite of a plethora of Ripper letters sent to the London police, the years of the terrible reign of the Ripper brought copycat killings in various parts of the land. One occurred in Halifax, and was simply the act of a drunken and deranged man, yet he gave as his motive the fact that he was copying Jack.

The Bradford murder is a different story, however, and the revolting details of the cuttings and maiming done to the boy's corpse do present a possibility that the Ripper had a trip up north. Cornwell links this trip north to the touring schedule of the Henry Irving company, and so to Sickert. Though slim logically, it cannot be discounted, as the letter in question says, 'I riped [sic] up a little boy in Bradford' and a letter of 16 January 1889 talks about 'my trip to Bradford'.

With all this in mind from the larger picture of a major criminal and his context, we still have an unsolved case here, and not much to go on. The circumstances are that John had been playing with friends on the morning of 27 December, and his mother saw him riding on a local milk cart (he was in the habit of doing this). But the boy never came home that night, and the family appeal described him as wearing a blue top coat, sailor cap and a plaid knickerbocker suit. He was almost eight, and didn't quite make it to his birthday just a week away.

His horribly mutilated body was found at the back of some nearby stables by one Joe Buckle. John had been savagely attacked, even to the extent of having his limbs cut off and placed next to his corpse. It was such a mess that Buckle, on first seeing the body, thought is was 'a heap of something propped up in the corner between the wall and the coach house door.' It was an attack with several of the hall-marks of the Ripper slayings: a piece of shirt was torn and tied around his neck; his heart had been pulled from his chest cavity and stuffed beneath his chin.

Of course, the dairyman was the first suspect, but nothing whatsoever was found on his property that could possibly incriminate the man. The only slight lead that was available turned out to lead nowhere: a copy of a Liverpool newspaper had been used in the wrapping around John's body, and only a few weeks earlier another Ripper letter had stated that he was currently in Liverpool, followed by a second letter from that port, only seven days before the Bradford murder.

The dairyman, Bill Barrett, was in the clear. The Liverpool theory came to nothing. This took some time, though, as he was patently connected to the boy in some way, and he was detained at the Town Hall. The lad had often been seen with Barrett, riding on the cart and so on. Gill had left Barrett on the fateful day, just before he made the last call at Walmer Villas.

Cornwell is convinced that other details in some Ripper letters point to Jack the Ripper as the killer, notably a sentence concerning his intention to attack boys now, after the prostitutes: he will, he says, 'rip them up the same way...any youth I see I will kill but you will never kitch me..put that in your pipe and smoke it.'

In the case of poor John Gill, do we have an unsolved case that is destined to be part of the Ripper 'canon' of crimes? The only slight link to previous thought on the Ripper and the

Liverpool connection may of course be in the life of prime suspect, James Maybrick. But following that link might lead to a long and fruitless pursuit. The fact remains that we have a Yorkshire connection of some interesting potential for Ripperologists. Moreover, the horrible murder of the innocent young boy is likely to remain unsolved.

Poor Barrett had his moment in the dock, though, the burning issue being the point that he passed very close to the spot where the boy died. It was on the Saturday evening, in front of the Borough magistrates. But all went well for him. A paper report at the time noted: 'after the police court examination, the prisoner had a long interview with his legal adviser and during the evening Barrett completely regained his coolness and cheerfulness which had been notably absent when interviewed earlier.' There we have it: the man was cleared and the puzzle remains.

CHAPTER SIX

Gamekeepers Shot: Bill Uttley and Bob Kenyon
1903

T he bare facts of this case are short, dramatic and baffling. On the wild moorland beyond Buckstones, the bodies of two gamekeepers were found: one, Robert Kenyon, was lying in what is known locally as a *gruff* –a gulley. The other, an older man called Bill Uttley, was found close to a landmark known as the Dinner Stone. Both had been shot through the back of the head, and the bodies were more than a mile apart.

Huddersfield railway station, where crowds walked and cheered to support Buckley.
The author

A man was charged, one Henry Buckley, of Moorside, but after a week-long trial at Huddersfield Police Court, he was cleared through lack of any sound evidence pointing to his guilt. Uttley's corpse was exhumed for a post-mortem, and this was done at Clough Lee; nothing significant came of this and the man was reburied in Marsden churchyard.

The murders took place north of Marsden, and the only known instigation of any potential trouble is that Kenyon and his father had been walking the moors, on duty, when they saw the figure of a man in the distance. The younger man, ex-soldier Robert Kenyon, son of William, a keeper, went in pursuit. William Kenyon clearly could not move so quickly, and the facts suggest that after killing the younger man, the murderer came after the old man, as he was a potential witness.

Kenyon was working as a teamster for Platts of Oldham, after a career serving in India. On the day he had taken off after the stranger, and not returned, his father worried and there was general concern for the young man's safety; father went out to search for him the next day, along with two young men called Quarmby and Garside. People went to ask Uttley's opinion of what had gone on, but he was not at home. At Ben Cut gruff they found old Uttley (known locally as Bill o' Marks). He was lying on his right side, with a gunshot wound behind one ear and some of his jacket cloth burnt. Superintendent Pickard was soon on his way out there from Huddersfield. It wasn't long before a £300 sum was offered for any information leading to an arrest.

Uttley was fifty-six, and left a widow and three children. Whatever happened to him, he had a gun; whereas young Robert had gone forward to investigate, leaving his gun with his father. So, when attacked, he would have had no weapon. His father searched the moors frantically until midnight, and he and his son had a mutual arrangement of coded firing to use as communication methods. The poor father had tried these things in vain, and in fact, learned later that he had passed the gulley where his son lay several times on that awful night.

Pickard and his team stayed to look around for some time on the moors. More details were given then to *Examiner*

The Magistrates' Court site today. The author

reporters, notably that thirty-six years earlier, one Mark Uttley, William's father, had also met his death from a gunshot wound, but that had been accidental. Another note concerned some workmen on the Buckstone road that day, who reported hearing several shots fired. They had assumed it was the usual gaming activities.

Through all this work, there was continual rain, and as the bodies were found so far apart, the team had a wide area to cover in that boggy area, known as the Brocken. Two constables and three other local men finally brought the body of young Kenyon back to Marsden.

Then, on 16 September, came the arrest of Henry Buckley. Sergeant Lee of Kirkburton and Sergeant Smith of

Saddleworth, arrested the man at his farm at Grains, and accompanied him to Huddersfield by train. He was a strongly built man of about forty, and made a point of letting it be known that he was a teetotaller, and that in previous years he had done some police duties in Oldham, mainly lamp-lighting. He had been noted as a man spotted on the Friarmere moors at the crucial time, but he said that he had seen two other men close by.

Late in the afternoon of 16 September, Buckley was in court, answering a charge of wilful murder. A slightly farcical element comes into the story here as there was no magistrate, and a man on horseback went out to find one; in the meantime, the press had plenty of time to study the suspect. Superintendent Pickard asked for Buckley to be remanded, and pointed out that the elder Kenyon had seen the accused in the place and at the right time. Buckley admitted to being on the moors at the time, but that he merely shot a grouse, having never seen the men, and returned home. He knew details such as the fact that he only winged the grouse; that his wife came out to fetch him home, and that he had plenty of witnesses to call if need be.

Buckley was remanded until the next Tuesday and there was no bail. When the press crushed into the Police Courts for the next appearance, Buckley had been brought by train from Wakefield, and Sergeant Lee was present again. There was a long and detailed discussion in the courtroom about the nature of the pellets on Uttley's body, and more importantly, some blood stains on Buckley's clothes. But forensic science could not ascertain the nature of the blood, and certain suspicions about the use of wadding with the pellets were asked, the defence hinting that old Uttley had perhaps caused his own death. All was eventually confusion and half-truth.

Buckley was cleared, to great applause. He exchanged hats with a temperance friend, after kissing his relieved wife, and walked out, with his friend's bowler covering rather more of his face in shadow than his normal flat cap. When he finally arrived home, there was a huge crowd waiting for him, to cheer, and at Greenacres Temperance Hall, he delivered what would now be called a media-friendly speech, even paying compliments to his Wakefield gaoler's kindness.

From there, the story of the double-murder passes into the records of the mysterious and unsolved, despite the finding of young Kenyon's watch, found wrapped in a red and white handkerchief up on the moors, which should have been a useful clue. In 1956 Granada Television made a programme filmed near Buckstones, and this included a crime reconstruction. Several celebrities were interviewed at the time, including Sir Linton Andrews, editor of the *Yorkshire Post*, a man who had been one of the first men to reach the crime scene when he was a seventeen-year-old cub with the former *Huddersfield Daily Chronicle*.

The fate of old Bill o'Marks and the young ex-soldier is very much a cold case in the files. One has to think how different things may have been if the young man had taken his gun. After all, he was a soldier, one who had seen Imperial service overseas, and he would have been a match for the enemy, one supposes.

CHAPTER SEVEN

An Outrage in Ilkley
Mary Learoyd, 1929

If ever there was a case of rumour and hysteria engulfing a small community, the murder of Mary Learoyd was it. After her body was found on a vacant plot of land at Sedbergh Park, on 25 August 1929, leads, suspicions, suspects and crowds all followed hotly on the story. Crowds gathered outside police stations; young people swore they had seen such things as a man in the woods foaming at the mouth. It was said that a madman had escaped from an asylum at Burley in Wharfedale. Many of these features typify the nature of extreme and brutal crime in a social context in which people were just coming to terms with the fact that such deeds were committed in places other than big cities.

The neighbourhood of Sedbergh Park, Ilkley. The author

Mary, aged thirty-six and a clerk, was naked when found, with her clothes scattered around the body in the grass. She had been severely beaten and her face was disfigured. Mrs Patchet, who found the body, had at first seen merely a leg protruding from the undergrowth and raised the alarm. Mary lived close by, and had been seen that day by many people, including some who recognised her at the library, and it is known that she left home at around eight o'clock to go to the cinema.

The hunt for the killer accelerated; bloodhounds were brought in, and there was even a chance that a fingerprint taken from a smudged, bloody handprint on Mary might lead to someone, but after being passed to police HQ at Wakefield, there was no progress there. People assembled in groups to watch and wait. An arrest was expected after the dogs were around, and other rumours had circulated; but suspects were few, and when leads appeared, they were short-lived enquiries, such as a hitch-hiker going to Lancashire, or a man who had been taken by taxi from Ilkley to Preston on that night.

Most intriguing of all are the sightings and overheard snatches of talk around the patch of waste land on that evening. Someone saw a man and woman talking by the telegraph pole which stands at the corner of the plot, close by the gate of Mrs Patchett. A girl, Alice Kears, even heard a scream from that area as she walked nearby at around 10.30. A sighting marked her presence with a man at around that time, and near the plot of land. The most tantalising shred of information is surely that in which Kears says she heard the girl's voice in the dark, say, 'Wait a minute and I'll kiss you.'

The more the story is studied, the more a climate of hysteria emerges. An example is the tale of a man who supposedly drowned himself in the River Wharfe, and that was not long after the murder. Was he full of a tormenting remorse? But rumours gradually subsided, after a poster was circulated offering a reward for information, and a verdict arising from the jury at Ilkley Town Hall decided on 'wilful murder by person or persons unknown.'

At the height of the moral panic, it had been spread around the community that there had been an arrest, and that a man from Ilkley was handcuffed and was at the station. A crowd of 400 people arrived and insisted on staying, not believing the official words that no arrest had been made that night. Obviously, the forces of the law were most disappointed at the lack of progress. The unfortunate Learoyd family must have felt damned: two other children of Louis Learoyd had died in 1918.

As with all these cases, there is room for some theorising, and Paul Langan, in his book on murders in Wharfedale, records some attempts in this way, including the inevitable search for local contacts. The first step is of course in asking about local men-friends, and Paul rightly speculates about a tryst with a local man, and a need for secrecy. One man who had sometimes given Mary a lift on his motorbike was ruled out. There has also been some discussion of the part played in the case by spiritualism, and some recent cases have shown that a medium can indeed sometimes provide answers or at least, some leads.

A final piece of criminal history that invitingly asks us to accept the possibility of some kind of closure here is that a daughter of one of the officers involved in the case wrote about a man who had done a similar murder in Leeds some years after the Learoyd killing; the man had been hanged for a murder, and apparently this man had been washing clean his bike to clean off blood stains, and this was on the night of the Ilkley murder.

The Learoyd case has been well covered by crime writers, and it invites the theorising we love to generate. Moreover, Mary was vivacious and very active locally, known by many. A photograph of her shows her laughing, with a dramatic gesture, tying a shoe on the rear of a wedding-car. She was quite tall and athletic, shapely and well groomed. It is easy to imagine that person being capable of extreme emotion, a passionate woman, perhaps likely to have 'involvements' and enjoy life so much that she takes the occasional risk, even with a stranger. That one of these might have been a fatal tryst in the darkness, is not inconceivable.

No-one has presented such a convincing scenario of this intriguing case as Tim Binding, in his book, *On Ilkley Moor*

(2001). He presents a suggestive and part-imagined narrative, combining several sightings of a short man with a limp, wearing a suit and carrying a raincoat, accompanying a young woman on that fateful night. He also makes it clear that there are questions about Mary Learoyd's lifestyle and habits which have a bearing on any theory that might be put forward. Binding's most enlightening insight is into the paradoxes of the young woman's life. On the one hand she seems to have had time to fill: long, aching hours in the day, moving from tea-room to family visits. But then, there was clearly some kind

Ilkley Parish Church, where Mary is buried. The author

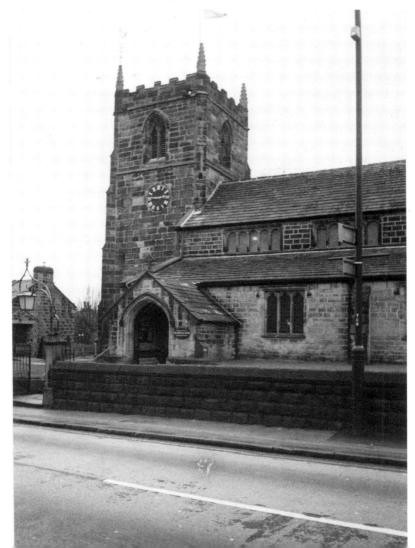

of liaison with a clergyman (married) and some odd behaviour around the time in the days before her death.

It is also a story with a massive media presence yet all that attention failed to pick up on the inner tensions and perhaps even the sexual frustration at the heart of the matter. We will never know the full facts, but so many people had perceptions, opinions and even reservations about Mary, that there will always be tantalising hints about her personal life, and these are hints that may help in any 'profiler' thinking on this celebrated case. For the time being, Tim Binding probably has the most insightful angle on the affair, and in some ways, this opens up new lines of thought.

Looking towards Ilkley Moor, one of Mary's regular haunts. The author

CHAPTER EIGHT

Otley Farmer Killed
1932

T o visit the Skipton Auction Mart today is to observe a busy, workaday place with Landrovers coming and going, and business people involved in their daily routine. It stands by the side of the Gargrave road out of town, about a mile past some very pleasant suburbs of the town. Only some scrutiny of local papers could reveal the dark, deadly events that took place there in 1932. On 23 March of that year, local farmer Joseph Swaine was found murdered in the toilets of the mart, his body being disregarded, and left there overnight after the killing.

A cleaner found the body the next day, barely alive. It must have been a slow, agonising death. He had been robbed and

Skipton Auction Mart. The author

left helpless, with a fractured skull and lying in his own blood. The poor man had not had the strength to cry for help.

Swaine's story is full of interest. If one visits the Chevin side of Otley centre, walking up towards Queen's Terrace, one can see the well-to-do Victorian home of his sweetheart, Gwen Forrest, who was only twenty-five; Swaine was much older – sixty-two in fact. He was thought to be a quiet man, unlikely to be involved in a fight. The theory at the time was that he had been attacked from behind and overpowered, then attacked in that small, enclosed space. Farcically, his false teeth were knocked out, and these were found on the day of the attack, nonchalantly placed in public view by some well-meaning passer-by, unaware that the owner was dying, just feet away.

Joseph Swaine was from a good family, and had been a tenant at Storriths Farm on the Otley Golf Club land. He had also worked in Otley and Burley. He had no known enemies, and police were sure that there was a gang of thugs and pickpockets around the cluster of towns in the valley, looking for opportunities like this one. However, though small, it was

Queen's Terrace and the Chevin beyond: where Swaine was due to lodge. The author

thought that Swaine would have put up a struggle. He was obviously building a new life for himself, with the young woman who was his fiancee, and was about to move near her in lodgings in Otley.

There were the usual desperate attempts to search for suspicious groups gathering at such places at race meetings and fairs around the north, but with no results. Again, the tracker dogs were called out, as they had been for Mary Learoyd. There were also the normal local rumours of casual

Otley Parish Church, where Swaine was buried in front of a large crowd. The author

labour in the area at the time. No fewer than 3,000 statements were gathered. Frustration and rumour followed, inevitably.

Skipton is the most unlikely place for such a brutal killing, being a place of great charm, with the castle, the riverside restaurants and hostelries for ramblers and fellwalkers. It is a farmer's centre as well, a place for the gregarious and sturdy Dalesman in town for the auction. The thought of a brutal criminal gang wandering around this place in search of a vulnerable older man to rob is almost beyond belief, particularly at that time. Naturally, the historian looks for other sources and motives. But very little becomes apparent here. In the end, the fact is that it was known that he carried large sums of money on his person. His fiancee had seen him the day before and was waiting for him to pay her a visit on the evening of the day of his death.

The robber gang theory persisted, but then comes an amazing twist to the story. This is in the shape of a remarkable character called Thomas Gaunt, twenty-four-years-old, staying in Bradford at the time in the Salvation Army hostel. Gaunt walked into Bradford police station and confessed to the murder. That would have been very neat and satisfactory for the investigation team, but it was not so simple. Gaunt's actions and words gradually became more and more unreliable and it was possible that he was deranged. He spoke of having an accomplice in the murder, but spoke in such a way that he would have appeared to be most unlikely to be involved by today's attitudes, but at the time, a Superintendent Blacker thought Gaunt worth hanging onto and investigating further.

In Skipton, Gaunt was charged with the murder of Joseph Swaine, and was on remand in Armley jail. From this point, his medical history creeps into the narrative and begins to have a persuasively questionable presence in the case. He had a long history of violence and derangement; he had always tended to be rootless and had no real evidence of a mental grasp on his sense of what was real and what was unreal. He could actually have been anywhere between the Midlands and Yorkshire on the day of the murder. His destiny was clearly to spend time in a mental asylum.

There we end, with no substantial theory of what happened that day at the mart. Imagining the scene, and accounting for the fact that Swaine was never seen and helped, it becomes probable that the atmosphere was noisy and packed. The

Swaine's fiancee's home. The author

sounds of the livestock as well as the hubbub from the people gathered there would have smothered any feeble cry for help. But nevertheless, it seems odd that no-one going to the toilets noticed anything suspicious. It is almost beyond belief that the afternoon of the mart would pass without some male visitor seeing the blood on the floor, or hearing a man desperately trying to make an audible sound.

The mart is in the dip of a hollow, with tracks sloping down to quite a small and compact space where the older buildings would have been huddled together. Everything in this thinking points to a noisy occasion, with drink in everyone's blood, and a slightly fevered atmosphere: just the kind of situation that an opportunist killer would take. Yet, equally, there is much we do not know about the man's personal life and relationships. Often the quiet men have most inner turmoil. Notably silent are the accounts of his emotional life, and also the inevitable stresses and strains on maintaining an affair of the heart with such a marked age difference. His interior life and reserve compare markedly with the 'confession' and need for recognition of the supposed killer.

But this is empty conjecture. The fact is that Swaine was killed in a nasty, violent manner, and we have no idea who did it, seventy two years on. His life, as far as it is known, appears to be peaceable, ordered and reasonably cheerful; he had no known involvements which might have led to enmity; no apparent feuds, vendettas or even jealousy may be invoked in this case. That silent emotional life may just provide the key, but it will never be known now.

CHAPTER NINE

Violent Death at the Moving Village
Fewston, 1938

Driving from Harrogate to Fewston today, along the Skipton road, there is a strong sense of time-travel. The roads down the valley side are steep and rough. A glint of light meets you through trees over the valley, and you pass a sparse scattering of dwellings, with plenty of earth around them. This is a community unchanged since this awful murder of one of its own – housewife Margaret Peel, beaten to death in her own home.

There is a silent, characterful churchyard by the side of the road as you travel down to Swinsty reservoir, and a silence.

Fewston, the church yard of St Michael and St Lawrence. The author

The silence is haunting, atmospheric. The place is hiding a secret, and it doesn't want to be disturbed. At the time of this death, the vicar testily defended this need for privacy, and he stood by his community, its probity, its unspoilt simplicity. It says a lot about this area when it is noted that the enquiry for the case was held well up the slope, on the Skipton road at the Hopper Lane Hotel, two miles from the church and the village centre.

This murder is one of those in which we find an obvious suspect, and so the mind naturally begins to criticise the actions taken in the investigation at the time. But this is unfair. There were many complicating factors here, and hindsight is a wonderful bringer of enlightenment, often too simplistic and wrong-headed. To understand the killing of Margaret Peel, it is necessary to trace a series of events on that day, and to keep in mind the nature and substance of this tiny place, where everyone was known and where routine was something observed and public. But this happened at a time when life was also less regimented and when the rule of the chronometers was limited. People could act with a degree of independence simply because there was trust, and there was also an acceptance of assumptions about people, coming perhaps from a more innocent time.

Ironically, the place has been called 'the moving village' as it is liable to subsidence, largely due to the construction of the Swinsty reservoir below the foundations. Although there are several more interesting stories, myths and tales of witchcraft around the village, and the intriguing thought of buried dwelling-places beneath the reservoirs, it is the murder of thirty-seven-year old Margaret Peel that has stolen the headlines.

At 9.30 one morning in spring, she was seen at work in the village shop. Her husband, Jesse, had left earlier that day to walk to work at the reservoirs, and was to go north of the village to Fewston reservoir. Around ten that morning, Mrs Peel was found dead on the floor of the shop, severely beaten, and in an atmosphere of chaos, blood and sheer mess and disorder.

It didn't take long for top detective and war hero D C S Huddleston to move in and start the search for the culprit. He

Fewston reservoir, where the tyre-lever was found. The author

even used the first ever two-way radio for communication in the field. Naturally, their priorities were to look out for strangers and travellers around the area, and to search for any clothing left out in the wild that would be blood-stained. But there was a main suspect – the husband.

Jesse's behaviour was slightly odd for a man in that situation and under such shock. Most prominent of all his surprising behaviour was that, on being taken to the murder scene, he actually stepped over his wife's body to get hold of something across the room. At first, he had also amazingly not entered the shop part of the building, but kept to the back room. His explanation for this was that he had not been told to do so by any officer. He also carefully checked all the places around the house and shop where there would be money – in the till and elsewhere. £12 in cash was missing. This behaviour was of course methodical, businesslike, sensible – and downright stunningly paradoxical to any suspicious mind. Things were complicated in this instance by the fact that one of the constables soon on the scene, P C Demaine, was Mrs Peel's brother. The other officer, P C Cartwright, who was the one who first saw Jesse come back to the shop, noted that the man never touched his wife's body.

Even worse for Jesse, blood was found on his clothes. Both his hat and coat were stained, and he said that this had happened when he was clearing brambles. Much of the suspicion then was confirmed by the logistics of Jesse's possible movements. Although he had been seen at work by colleagues, it was quite feasible for him to have walked back home by a quiet path known as Back Lane, and to have done the murder, then walked back to work, all unobserved. It looked bleak for him when a tyre lever was found in the Fewston reservoir and was thought to be the murder weapon. This had been hard work – an electro-magnet was used, after eight days of dragging the waters.

The husband was charged but at trial in Leeds the case for the prosecution was thin. Everything they had was patently circumstantial and there was no solid evidence. The real cul de sac in the charges against him was the lack of any motive. Why on earth would he do such a thing? They were well known as a happy couple. No villagers could say anything about rows or altercations – or even any obvious bad feeling. They never had a tiff. Even more supportive of his innocence was the lack of any logical link between the amount of blood on his clothing and the bloodbath in the room of the killing. Mr Paley Scott, K C, described the case against Jesse as 'trifling'. Now, from the viewpoint of the twenty-first century, we have to note what DNA forensics would have achieved.

There was public applause when he was acquitted and he returned to live in the village. Not long after he died on the road. All evidence, including a statement made by a police officer with Peel when he died in Harrogate, confirms that any rumour about a death-bed confession is untrue. We have another mystery here.

The best gauge of the scale of shock and abhorrence aroused in the area by this case is the actions of the vicar, the Reverend Cubbon, of the church of St Michael and St Lawrence, who was notably upset by the arrival of sick crime tourists, eager to see the gruesome spot where the deed was done. The Washburn valley had never had such a bad press and such a disruption to its placid way of life.

It was a Miss Ethel Marston who found the body, calling into the village shop, after going to the Communion service. She was friendly with Maggie Peel, being a teenager at the time, and a sociable person. She reported that she knocked and went in, calling out Mrs Peel's name, and then found her lying on the floor. It was a nasty affair; the victim had been struck eleven times on the head. She had been attacked from behind, her skull fractured. Ethel ran out and screamed murder.

To spend some time in that silent village now is almost to sense those screams still cutting the air. It is indeed the last

Hopper Lane Hotel on the Skipton road. The inquest was held here. The author

place on earth one would expect such a brutal killing to have taken place. The 'moving village' had been moved in quite another way, and somehow, the dark history of witchcraft and local myth associated with the work of local writer Edward Fairfax seems to cast a shadow over the landscape. In such a matter-of-fact workful community, it seems unfitting to mention myths and superstition, yet somehow those words fit well with this particular mystery in such an idyllic part of rural Yorkshire. Previous writers on the village and the surrounding countryside have made much of the particular brooding melancholy felt as one spends time there: it has the quiet inscrutability of a scene in fiction, and it would be an easy matter to describe the mysteries of this violent death in such terms, but the remaining feeling on contemplating such a killing in the place of beauty is sheer disbelief: the old familiar words of crime fiction: *it couldn't happen here.*

Yet it did, and the full facts are still unrecorded.

CHAPTER TEN

Murder of a Child
Bradford 1938

In 1969, the *Yorkshire Post* reported that the case of Phyllis Hirst was still open, and that police were asking for people to help and come forward with information. The reference is to a murder of 1938, when the body of eight-year-old Phyllis was found dead and sexually assaulted in a back alley near Little Horton Green, by Sarah Johnston, as she walked her dog.

This is a major murder story, with several false leads and a very intricate narrative of reporting and theoretical interpretation of possible events. The bare facts of the immediate actions taken on finding the girl's body are these. First, she was found not far from where her father, Arthur, had known she had gone out to play. He searched a string of lanes and alleys when she had not returned home at the expected time. Then she was found by Mrs Johnston, who ran to St Luke's hospital, but the girl was dead, and the next step was a matter of pathology.

Phyllis had been killed elsewhere and brought to that place. D S O'Hara led the enquiry, and soon contacted some scientific advisers, notably Dr Lloyd of the Bradford College of Technology chemistry department, and Mr W Warburton, a textile expert. This work established that she was just still alive when put down on the ground in the lane. The only lead at this point was a sighting of a man on a bicycle carrying something in a bag over the

Phyllis Hirst – from a photo circulated at the time. Laura Carter

Savile Park, Halifax, where the suspect was seen by three people, on a bus. The author

handle-bars. This was a slender shred of enquiry, but it was a start. Someone had noted that the bag carried was 'a sack of irregular shape' – a tantalisingly inviting clue to link the body to this man – particularly as there was brick dust under her finger nails, and no such bricks where she lay when found. The cyclist became the major suspect, and much was known about him: he was short, around five feet five inches; he had long black hair and was of slight build, clean shaven and wore a raincoat. He was seen later, going towards the city, and this time without a bag over the handle-bars.

It was a case with a very high media profile, and the sense of outrage in the city was great: more than a thousand people came out to her funeral on Manchester Road, at the Central Mission Hall. Most heart-rending was the sight of Phyllis's friends from her Brownie troop along the road to Queensbury cemetery.

A contemporary photograph shows something of the nature of the lane where the girl was found: there are high stone walls along both sides, and a considerable distance to the nearest house. The lane itself is several hundred yards long, and the precise spot where she was found is below a five-foot solid wall, making a dark shadow beneath. Sarah Johnston stated at the inquest that the girl was naked to the waist, and had a brown beret on her face. The time of the sighting was at ten thirty on a Friday night, and Sarah Johnston saw no vehicles nearby as she walked, nor any other people walking in the vicinity.

Phyllis had had tea with the Bayliss family of William Street and left them at around 5.30 to go out and play. The Chief Constable pointed out that there had been several cases reported of men accosting young girls around the Sterling Street district. A man who had given Phyllis some cash to buy sweets was tracked down, interviewed and cleared. Hundreds of statements were taken, and people had brought a large quantity of clothing to the Town Hall, hoping to help find the missing clothes, but no progress was made.

Leads began to proliferate as the net was more widely spread, and a notable instance was a connection to Skircoat Green, Halifax. A man seen behaving strangely and also fitting a description circulated linked to the Hirst murder, was reported by bus passengers. A man was seen boarding a bus at Horton Park Avenue, and it was thought that the Halifax sighting was the same man.

But then, as time passed, the sightings multiplied and by 11 November, descriptions were issued of three men seen around Little Horton Lane talking to little girls: one was aged fifty to sixty; one was thirty to thirty-five and one around twenty. There was even a police search of an empty house in Portland Street after a woman reported seeing a face looking through a window from the inside. Things were becoming desperate, and nothing material or substantial established.

Skircoat Green. Another clear sighting of the same man was made here. The author

A significant step forward seemed to be achieved when a taxi driver, Herbert White, gave a close description of a van seen parked at the end of the lane where the girl's body was found. He caught a glimpse of a spoked wheel and a bonnet. He also saw a high canopy, maybe tarpaulin. Intriguingly, this was only forty minutes before the body was found. She was certainly brought there from the place of the murder, and a bike links the sightings.

Throughout October and November, possibilities continued, many of the theories being no more than wishful thinking or desperate measures so that something was being seen to be done. The papers were keen to make the most of any hint, such as the announcement that the killer might have been a woman. The general thinking was that mentally troubled and distraught women might be likely to do such awful things. 'Cases of mental derangement leading women to commit such crimes have been known in recent years' said the *Yorkshire Post*. In other words, D S O'Hara was at the end of his tether and the papers wanted anything, however slender, to report.

Finally, before everything levelled out into a sense of defeat, a Mrs Mary Anne O'Brien, later in November, came forward to say she had seen a girl trying to reach up and jump onto a bike on Sterling Street. 'She walked away with him and they turned up Manchester Road.' She said. Following this a man in Liverpool was interviewed, and the only thing about him that we ever knew was that he rode a bike.

Of all the unsolved Yorkshire cases, the murder of little Phyllis Hirst is the most informative about that semi-mythical social history older people talk about when kids could play out and be safe, and that doors were left open. The fact is that in this particular neighbourhood of Bradford, Mr Hirst, unemployed painter, learned the hard way that there were men of dubious character wandering those dark alleys and they were out to maim, rape and kill.

At the time, snippets of popular psychology about 'loners' and 'troubled souls out alone' were bandied about, but in the end, this case remains an enigma, and a search of the contemporary accounts of the enquiry lead one to the conclusion that good solid police work was done, but there were too many small leads and more possibilities than solid facts.

Much of the current reporting of the story evokes a more innocent time, when the resources of law and investigative procedures were limited and in some ways doomed to fail, as the knowledge just was not there. Consequently, short reports regularly appeared in the Yorkshire papers eager to make a 'story' of every theory put forward by an academic or a noted psychologist.

These shreds of half-truth only served to cloud the waters even more, and today the obscurity is perhaps more intense than ever in this terrible murder.

CHAPTER ELEVEN

The Body in the Park
1953

From 12 June 1953, Bradford police were very sure what sort of man they were looking for in a murder investigation. He had been seen running across a golf course near Bowling Park that evening, around half past five. He was distinctive in many ways, mainly because he was 'knock-kneed' and was said to have a long nose. But he was between thirty and thirty-five, slim, with brown hair, and was wearing a fawn raincoat. He was wanted to help with enquiries concerning the murder of Catherine Ogden, a married woman with five children. Her story is soon told but her death not easily explained, and a study of it leads only to a frustrating series of speculations.

She was also known as Kitty Bannon, and lived on Hubert Street, off Leeds Road. That day she had gone with a man in a taxi to Bowling Park. After a phone call to police from Odsal Top, her body was found in undergrowth at an area of the park known as Lover's Walk. Police thought she had been killed in the afternoon and dragged into the bushes, which were near a tennis court used by a local college. When found by D S Naylor at seven that evening, nothing was found that suggested any motive of robbery.

Where do we go from here in considering this case? At the end of the trail was an open verdict. She had been strangled, but there was no certainty that a murder had taken place. Catherine

Catherine Ogden – from a photo circulated at the time. Laura Carter

Ogden is a puzzling personality in many ways, from what little we know. Two photographs of her suggest two very different people. One shows her smiling demurely, every inch the nice mum. She has her hair very neatly cut and combed and wears a flowery blouse. In the other, we have a woman wearing national health spectacles, with hair in rollers and rather unkempt. Her lips suggest a nervous, repressed individual. These are Jekyll and Hyde images. We know only that she took a taxi to a place where lovers met and had illicit sex; we know the man with her had fair hair and carried a fawn raincoat. After that it is mostly conjecture.

At a press conference, when asked about the murder, Superintendent Rushworth was defensive: 'Who says it is murder? We have never said so.' So the search went on, in and beyond the city. More and more, the theory was that the killer was local. The obvious conclusion here would be that he was a married man and he had a lot to hide and even more to lose by going public in such circumstances. Questions about whether there was a struggle, and they fought? Did the man use too much strength and do more than intended to the woman?

The more reason is applied to the case, the less certainty arises from the few facts. Even people nearby who perhaps would have been expected to see or hear suspicious sounds or movements, did not. Harold McMara, the tennis court attendant, was having some tea from five to half past five, and when he returned to duty (which would have been around the time when something was going on in Lover's Walk), he reported nothing unusual or remarkable. Bolling High School girls had played tennis and people had strolled and walked their dogs that afternoon, and somewhere in the midst of all this a woman was killed.

There was a massive search. Leave was cancelled in the city police. They were looking for something as elusive as the victim's own self: here we have a woman separated from labourer John Ogden. She was as far as we know healthy. The detectives even dodged questions about a sexual motive. It almost seems as if there was a sense of dishonour, disgrace, or some unthinkable shaming involved in saying much in public about the woman.

We are left with a lovers' tryst and a secret meeting that led to a killing. Catherine was thirty-six, and she had had a life of duty and responsibility. Now here she was walking out with a man, going in search of a quiet time with him – this in a period when such 'brief encounters' were necessarily discreet in such a moral atmosphere. It must also be recalled that she had been, like so many, a mother in wartime and experiencing rationing. Then her marriage had turned sour. She was an older woman: her partners would have been married men with similar needs. But something went terribly wrong that afternoon. Taking a taxi out to such a quiet place also implies determination to be alone. Perhaps they had some important decisions to talk over; maybe promises were made and broken.

Ultimately, we have a sad death of a woman looking for love and companionship. Instead of this, she found someone capable of taking her life from her. It may be that the call from Odsal was a pathetic and desperate act of remorse, from a killer who had lost control, gone too far. But his identity remains a mystery.

Most likely, this is yet another of those stories of brief encounters that involve some risk: this risk was fatally miscalculated.

CHAPTER TWELVE

Emily Pye
1957

Walking down Gibbet Street in Halifax today, one walks through the heart of the town's Asian community. Though the street names remain, and reflect British industrial history, there is also a mosque and a general sense of life on the streets. But surviving in the centre of all this is a small corner shop on the end of Rhodes Street, and back at Whitsun time in 1953, eighty-year-old Emily Pye owned that shop. It was her life: she was well known and well liked. It is easy to imagine her dealing out sweets, a kindly old lady in a close community.

But that Saturday, with many local people away for a short holiday, Emily was brutally attacked and murdered in her back room. She was found under a rug on the floor, with her head battered in. Her niece and her husband had called to invite Emily out for the day, and become suspicious when there was no answer.

There were many things standing in the way of the enquiry – not least the fact that there had been severe weather on the day of the murder. A thunderstorm could easily have shielded

Emily Pye's shop, off Gibbet Street.
The author

The back room in Rhodes Street where the killing took place. The author

any cries or noise from the back of the shop. There were very few witnesses and not much to go on for the top detectives called up north from Scotland Yard. It was indeed a high profile case.

The attack must have been an ordeal. The killer had taken money from the till and maybe knew of the existence of more cash hidden in the back room. But it was never found. An informant who knew Emily has stated that the old lady always used to pay for everything with coppers or small silver, particularly silver threepenny bits, as one lady told me: a worker to whom Emily used to visit to pay cash. Her habits were those of a person with odd habits regarding money, perhaps suggesting that she stored money – notes in fact – on the premises, while existing on small change. After all, we know that she 'never went anywhere' and there is a habit of mind in parts of West Yorkshire that has played its part in the stereotype niggardly Tyke. Was Emily Pye a miserly character, careful with the pennies? The behaviour of the killer suggests someone who strongly suspected that the old lady had notes stashed away somewhere on the property. Why else lock them both in the back room and beat the victim? The final murder may have been the result of frustration at not having forced any information from her, and then of course, the witness had to be silenced. It seems highly likely that Emily knew her killer.

But the case gave the media a good time. The detectives were dashing figures, notably Herbert Hannam. A photograph of the time in the *Courier* shows Hannan as a dapper, romantic figure, something of an intellectual. He was interviewed as a figure from *Boy's Own* stories rather than as purely a methodical policeman. However, searches and wider enquiries brought nothing definite. The shop was not far from the main road to Lancashire, and Gibbet Street leads to the centre of town and to a junction close to the exits for Bradford and for the moors towards Denholme and Howarth. But nothing came from such enquiries as notes on hitch-hikers or lorry drivers.

The affair reached almost mythic status in the area for some years, as the name 'Emily Pye' became synonymous with the fear of unsolved murder and with the menace at large to innocent and vulnerable citizens. This was intensified by the fact that Emily had such a good reputation in the community. At one time when she had been ill and had closed the shop when she was in hospital, she had told her niece that she thought a lot of the customers, and ran the shop more as a hobby than anything else. All the more horrible, then, that such a warm-hearted and sociable woman should die in that way.

A photograph taken of Emily Pye when she went to enjoy a Park Ward old folks' treat show as a round-faced, very good-humoured woman smartly dressed and with an open, approachable face. She had been asked about the dangers of living alone, but not shown much concern. Everything about her personality suggests a person who is happy to help others, and feel the satisfaction of helping the neighbourhood, knowing her customers and doing what all local shops do: cater for individual needs and order things when in demand.

Such heartless killings of vulnerable old women are definitely a classification of crime, as there are many such cases (notably the murder of Constance Aris in Cheltenham in 1985 which has some similarities to this) but the statistic of most murderers being known by their victims has a powerful application in this case. Everything about this murder in such an ordinary, peaceful neighbourhood led to that mythology that surrounds any place in which a killer is 'abroad' but never found.

On occasions, in apparently simple and straightforward attacks and killings of this kind, local knowledge provides the ultimate key; but most troubling about the death of Emily Pye is the lingering thought that the murderer is more likely to have been from the streets around the shop than a passing opportunist in need of a few pounds from the till.

CHAPTER THIRTEEN

A Killing at Christmas
Barkisland 1965

Vicky Williamson was a mender at the woollen mill in Barkisland, and on 23 December 1965 she had done some shopping in Elland. Surprisingly, she was walking from Elland back home, carrying her shopping bags, when some unknown assailant dragged her from the road into fields near Wood End Lane, Zechariah Wood, not far from the Branch Road Inn. Vicky had been violently attacked. Professor Polson, the forensic scientist who reported on the case, stated that there were many cuts and bruises around her face, and that she had been strangled. Vicky was lightly built, and not a young woman, hardly robust and able to fight back.

The entire area between Greetland and Brighouse is sparsely populated, and the lanes and slopes are quiet places, providing good cover for anyone with a nefarious intent. Vicky was taking a risk walking alone in that area. Branch Road, for instance, is narrow, and darkened by overhanging trees. But even so, there are puzzling questions here. The toughest one is why she was dragged and lifted over walls and across an extensive area to the place where she died. One would expect a sexual attack but this was not the case, in spite of the telling detail that the two jumpers she wore were pulled over her head. She was killed close to where she lived, and if robbed, little was taken. The presents she bought were not

Vicky Williamson – from a contemporary drawing. Laura Carter

expensive ones, and were scattered around her body when found.

The inquiry involved visits to over a thousand workplaces, and 2,000 local men were interviewed by officers. The clothing found, the sightings and even some of the details of her movements, did not add up to anything that could be followed constructively.

There were sightings, and important ones. A man had been seen leaving Zechariah Wood after eight that night, and had eventually walked to the Saddleworth road. Drivers had seen a young man wearing distinctive clothing that night, too. Clothes and footwear had been discarded within a mile of the killing, and there was an identikit picture issued. This showed a man quite short, with light brown hair but with an average face. Nothing was achieved with this. A search was carried out, statements taken, and a hundred detectives were on the case.

Vicky had been seen carrying the bags at about half past six. This sighting turned out to be only half a mile from the place of attack. Things were slightly confused by the fact that glass was found on the road, and for a while, the thinking was that she had been killed by a hit and run driver, and dragged off the road. This was incorrect, as it turned out. Quite a lot was known about her movements that day, but there were puzzles. For instance, shopkeepers in Elland recalled her buying things, but not tobacco, and quite a lot of tobacco was found

The Greetland road, showing the woods where Vicky was found. The author

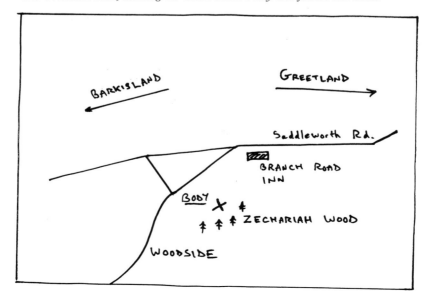

near her body. Where did she buy it then? Why did she walk home with that weight?

For the two young boys who found the body, this was a shock, and local feeling ran high. As luck would have it, capital punishment had only recently been abolished, with the last two executions taking place in Liverpool and Manchester in April and August 1964. So just a year or so before this terrible killing, the death deterrent was in force. Naturally, this was in the minds of many Yorkshire people after Vicky's death. An MP was sent a telegram, as Matthew Spicer reports, saying 'Goodwill to all men is neither in our hearts nor on our lips this season' and asked him to bring the politician responsible for passing the bill to Barkisland 'to find out what villagers think of his no-hanging bill...'

One general point should be made here, too. The area in that triangle of Elland, Greetland and Barkisland has always been, in historical terms, a place where opportunist crimes take place. There were two notable ones in the Edwardian period. It has a lot to do with the proximity of main routes across the Pennines, and maybe this is a pocket of low resistance and non-defensible space, as some sociologists might put it. Poor Vicky Williamson didn't help the cause of public safety in that landscape when she took the walk. In fact, her reasons for the walk, and the purchases she had made may be part of the answer to this particular unsolved case. She may even have bought the tobacco from a traveller, and he may have turned nasty for some reason.

Once again, more questions than answers are raised.

Part III

Around Leeds

CHAPTER ONE

Baffling Batley Mystery 1881

John Critchley had powerful connections in West Yorkshire. His father was a JP and his brother a magistrate. His home was no less a place than Batley Hall. But something about John's lifestyle made him a stranger to his home and family. What exactly his habits involved remains a puzzle, but various aspects of his death open up dramatic and sensational questions. The death was the result of foul play, and almost certainly murder.

As with many of these mysterious deaths, the material circumstances of the body when discovered indicate a whole raft of possibilities. He was found on a doorstep on Batley High Street, by two miners on their way to work at the West End pit; moreover, John Critchley's corpse was in a sack, and the doorstep was that of his former lover, Mary Wigglesworth. This was on 30 May 1881, and the place where the sack was put, only half on the step and half on the road, was ironically a butcher's shop. One has to think that, given the state of the body, it was a sick joke. In fact, doubly so when we consider that someone thought it fitting to present the man's body to his one-time sweetheart.

The state of the body gives rise to some unsavoury thoughts. First, he was half naked, wearing only trousers and a hat. The feet were tied together and the torso trussed, with the hands over the chest. Although there were no pronounced signs of beatings or abrasions on the body, most of the body mass was swollen. As it was found at half past four in the morning, and had not been seen by the policeman on his beat in the area when he passed the shop at two-thirty, it was easy to say when it was 'delivered'. The sight was a real shock for miner Peter Kelley and his son so early in the morning.

But pathologists were sure that he had been dead for a day or so, so he was killed elsewhere, and the connection with Mary Wigglesworth had ended some weeks before. It is at this point that the complexity sets in. Initially, murder was not necessarily the case, and more urgent questions were naturally related to the reason why the body was dumped where it was. Instinctive reactions would want to construct some sort of argument implicating the Wigglesworth family. Had Critchley done her wrong? Was there a score being settled here? Much about the state of the body suggests a slow, almost ritual killing, judging by the way he was tied.

If it was not murder but manslaughter of some kind, and Critchley had died in rather embarrassing circumstances, so extreme that companions would not have wanted anything made public, then it is just conceivable that his choice of lifestyle involved activities and behaviour that would have included dangerous and life-threatening experience. If anything in this context could be called a clue, it had to be what was found on the body. Intriguingly, there were photographs of Mary and some tickets from a pawnbroker. But, as David Goodman makes clear in his discussion of the case (see *Foul Deeds and Suspicious Deaths in Leeds* – bibliography) then nothing tangible came from these sources. Goodman also makes the very relevant point that associates would have been reluctant to come into the open with stories or evidence. Everything points to Critchley living life on the edge, a rake, shiftless and nomadic. In some ways, bearing in mind his wealthy family and their local status, what little we know of him hints at the possibility of him squandering money drinking and gambling, and it looks highly likely that he mixed with the wrong crowd. Certainly, the *Yorkshire Post* statement made about the case uses the phrase, 'companions of his wretchedness' who 'got rid of the body in an ingenious manner.'

If the latter point is true, then it still leaves open the teasingly seedy and iniquitous probability that the death had a connection with Wigglesworth. When we read about the inquest at the Victoria Hotel today, we want to put forward questions about the Wigglesworth connection – why he still had her photographs on him, and what exactly had been the story of this man's decline from regular work as a card maker down to skid row, a middle-aged man most likely killed slowly and brutally, perhaps as a way of settling a score.

CHAPTER TWO

Kate Summerfield
1911

In the new business district of Leeds, extending from the Headrow in the north, down through brasseries and cafes to Wellington Street, it is difficult to catch any glimpses in the architecture of the old Leeds of the Victorian to inter-war years. Wellington Street, stretching from the Majestic and City Square all the way out to the impressive Yorkshire Post buildings, was once at the heart of the more nefarious activities of the city's underclass. In fact, along the river from the Aire and Calder wharf along to The Calls was also, traditionally an area harbouring criminals, and in those dark yards and alleys it was not wise to travel alone. Even as recently as the 1950s and 1960s, the streets around the Corn Exchange could be dangerous at night. Across from these areas was a set of dark courts and public houses off Boar Lane.

In the early years of the twentieth century, one of the trades plied around Wellington Street was prostitution, and the sad tales of the denizens of these mean streets provide plenty of interest to the historian of crime. One of the most well-known unsolved cases concerns Kate Summerfield, a prostitute living in Miller's Square, a place that does not exist now. Then, as she began a new life after a failed marriage, partnered by one John Studholme, a general labourer, she may have tried to make a living from scratch, but her drink problem was still with her.

Kate had made a living on the streets, and her drinking habits had always meant that she would struggle financially. When she settled in the new flat in 1910 with a respectable man friend, it must have seemed a bright new start.

But here she was, now forty-years-old, still accepting most of her clients from the less well-off. She was on the lower rungs of the ladder of what may be called a 'career' in this context. As Studholme was unemployed, there was a point at which things became desperate, and it is easy to imagine their plight. She knew only one way of earning a large sum of money – to go out trawling for customers more frequently and with more determination, although it has always been known what a high-risk profession that of 'hooker' is, and more so in a large industrial town with problems of urban crime and transient populations.

The area today, close to where Miller's Square once stood. The author

Wellington Street, Leeds. The author

Yet none of this basic sociology counts for anything when eviction or starvation become real possibilities. So Kate set about her work and found a client who was clearly willing to pay very well indeed for a full night's entertainment. But this would have to be in the Miller's Square flat. Studholme finally agreed to this, and booked himself into the Adelphi lodging house.

At ten the next morning, after trying to wake her up, Studholme, now very concerned about Kate, forced entry and went in, to find a sight almost as horrific as the Ripper killings in Whitechapel not that long before. Kate had been bludgeoned to death and was on the bed, her wrists strapped to the bed posts so that she was in the shape of a cross. She was still in some underwear, and had been stabbed seventeen times. It all had the marks of being a frenzy attack, and her skull was fractured. A knife was found in the kitchen, but this turned out not to be the murder weapon. Death had been caused by asphyxiation. Before the actual killing, though, she had been attacked with a brick, and the brick was still in the room, with strands of her hair and blood still on it. There was also a whisky bottle in the room, so clues were many and a narrative of Kate's last night was soon put together. Studholme could help with this, and he said that Kate had met the client at the flat, then gone out drinking with him. She had been seen by a shopkeeper earlier in the evening, and she spoke to him, mentioning the man back at the flat. She was also seen much later on, and was by then very much inebriated. The man with her was seen too, but there was no description taken, or perhaps given. It was dark and late. Leeds around midnight in the drinking areas has always been a rowdy and confusing place. The streets where the pubs were tend to lead off ill-lit courts, such as the several taverns off Briggate.

Studholme raised the alarm, and the police operation began. George Tarry, the Chief Constable, put D S Handley in command of the investigation. The time of death could be placed only between midnight and ten am. Forensics at that time could do no better. Most informative would have been the evidence that much that was done to her was effected after

The Ship Inn: a favourite place of Studholme's The author

A yard off The Calls. A typical spot for Victorian 'ladies of the night' The author

her death. Today, this would give rise to a detailed psychological profile, as the hands were tied after death, and the crucifix shape is surely indicative of the tendency of sex murderers to like to communicate something about themselves at a death scene.

All we are left with is a rabid, frenzied murder of a poor prostitute, a woman extremely drunk, doing distasteful work in sheer desperation and straitened circumstances. Studholme had to be the prime suspect, but his alibi worked out; he had been seen and witnesses made statements to verify his presence both at the lodging-house and in the café and public house he had named.

It would have been the kind of murder which, at the time, would have given rise to 'Ripper' lines of thought and fears of more such murders to come. Fortunately, it was not repeated. Yet the pattern of the killing has all the hallmarks of that specific version of sex killing we associate with both the Whitechapel murders and with the later Yorkshire Ripper. In 1911, in that part of a rapidly-expanding northern city, it was fatal to fall behind with the rent, and that was the initial source of this whole bloody and violent tale of murder. It was a social climate that made thousands of Studholmes and Summerfields; mostly, these people are anonymous and drift into a textless history. In this case, we know names and characters, and we know one tragic tale. Poverty pushed over the first domino, and the last one to fall was a death sentence.

Women like Kate operated alone, and in her case the independence her work brought her explains a great deal about the chancy nature of her life: perhaps a combination of danger and excitement says it all. The 'game' was always going to be short, but it made the women existing on it live on the edge in an urban community always likely to contain criminal elements. As Henry Mayhew's London prostitute, speaking of the situation in 1850 said, 'Many a poor girl has been ruined in this house ... get used there indeed, and you are life-ruined.'

In Leeds in particular, we know quite a lot about their treatment, thanks to work done by the historian J J Tobias, who has pointed out that between the years 1857 and 1875 the number of women proceeded against under the Vagrancy Act averaged around forty per year. By 1875, closer to Kate's world, there were sixty-seven prosecutions. As there are figures for women of 'good' as opposed to 'unknown' character prosecuted in these years, it partly explains why and how Kate became what at the time would have been a 'fallen woman.'

The feeling on reading this back-street tragedy is that of shining a torch into a very dark place and feeling a shiver of fear.

CHAPTER THREE

The Margaret Schofield Case
Dewsbury 1931

Every cold murder case has its peculiarities, and its own atmosphere, be it certain weather conditions, or merely the terrain around the murder scene. The murder of fifty-six-year-old Margaret Schofield on 2 January 1931 had these elements in the extreme. The night was very dark and cold; street lighting was poor and a mist was around Dewsbury. Then, the discovery, by a store manager, Mr Sprentall, just before eleven in that evening, was the grotesque sight of two bare legs in the moonlight.

Maggie Schofield, a woman with no fixed address, had been beaten to death in a yard only a hundred yards from where a police constable stood on duty. Mr Sprentall approached and saw her body lying face downwards. She was naked from the waist down and more clothing had been taken from her upper body. By her side was a blood-stained beer bottle. This turned

Dewsbury on a bright winter night, at the time of the murder. Laura Carter

out to be the murder weapon. But, amazingly, there was still a tiny spark of life in the woman as the constable looked at the scene. This was as he removed a gag from her mouth – just a piece of old rag.

She was rushed to hospital, but died before arrival at Dewsbury Infirmary. There were to be many enigmatic aspects of this case as the story of her last night alive unfolded. Maggie was well known to the police, as the reporter for the *Yorkshire Post* put it in 1961, she was 'a woman of questionable moral character' and so it seems highly likely that she met her killer for reasons connected with their walk to this quiet yard, naturally almost certainly sexual motives.

But we have to pause, as it has never been the case that investigation thought this to be a male killer. Many blows had been struck, but none of them was consistent with a wound given by a person of any real strength, and the skull had not been broken, in spite of these blows. Also, Maggie's coat was missing: it was most distinctive, a fur coat trimmed at the neck and cuffs. It must have seemed like a proper break-through when this garment was found in the Calder on 5 January near to the Aldams Road bus station. That place was only a hundred yards from the murder scene. Previously, it was assumed that if the killer were a man, and thus with plenty of blood on him, and most likely carrying a woman's coat through town late at night, he would have been noted by several bystanders. But that was not the case.

There were many peculiarities about the killing; by the body there was a pile of celery-tops. This is exactly the sort of bizarre detail which leads to the wild-goose chase. Other developments led the investigation astray; a man came forward with an iron perambulator axle bar which had been found hidden nearby. But this was not consistent with the wounds on the head. Forensic investigation demonstrated that another weapon had indeed been used, in addition to the beer bottle.

As with all murders involving victims from the poorer areas of a town, the Schofield case meant that police had to undertake a systematic search of the seedier and more run-down areas of Dewsbury, the places with the cheap lodging-houses. This work did result in several of Maggie's friends being found and interviewed, but with no result. Of course, Scotland Yard officers were on the scene. C I Collins and D S Ayto arrived, and on a foggy northern day, they visited the crime scene and had a briefing with the local detectives.

One important lead appeared to be the sighting of a man on a bus that night, a man with blood on him. But he was tracked down and spoken to, without any doubts cast upon his explanation. There were a few clues to lines of enquiry, such as a Burnley newspaper found, and a man was located, then eliminated from the enquiry. Another man, from Ossett, spent over fourteen hours with the police before being allowed to leave.

An officer referred to the victim as a 'harmless unfortunate' and the fact is that her funeral attracted a large crowd. There were more than five thousand people at Dewsbury Cemetery. This led to one churchman condemning the 'morbid curiosity' of local people. He noted that 'Had the woman died a natural death there would not have been half as many to see her buried.' He had a point there, but the fact is that it was a high-level enquiry, demanding lots of man-hours for solid police work.

As with other cases, such as that of Joseph Swaine, there were 'confessions'. One, by one Joseph Coonan, a destitute cobbler, in Doncaster, proved to be a lie. Then, ten years after the killing, a man went to the police in Ashby de la Zouche, Leicestershire, and confessed, saying he killed her with a bottle. This 'confession' was by a person with severe mental problems, but it is a stunning fact that he was in front of the magistrates four times during this process of confession and examination. The case is similar to that of the man Gaunt in the Swaine murder: a deranged man coming forward, somehow needing to be noticed, and entering vicariously into the story.

After taking and combing through over two hundred statements, police had a man who had been in Maggie's company whom they wanted to trace. They never did; and so we have another murder mystery, taking place on a cold night in a dark corner: a place where only desperate and reckless people would take a stranger. Margaret Schofield paid the ultimate price for that risk.

CHAPTER FOUR

Widow Killed at Bramley
1945

Annie Nichols, a sixty-three-year-old widow, kept a shop in Bramley, a settlement on the hillside above Kirkstall Abbey and the Aire in one of its more picturesque moods. But there was nothing scenic about this death: it was a strangling, merciless and brutal.

She was found dead in the back room behind her shop in Broad Lane, and had been beaten about the head as well as strangled; she was small and frail and it would not have been a difficult task to overpower her and then take her life. Annie was also hard of hearing and her eyesight was poor. Rarely has there been such a vulnerable and defenceless victim in a murder.

Unusually, the murder took place in the morning, between eight and nine. The report in the newspaper at the time makes the valuable point that the attacker would have escaped into a crowd of commuters very easily. The back room, however, had a small table from which she was in the habit of serving early customers, often at half past six. She must have sold the morning paper from this small table; and in fact her body was found lying back in that small chair where she would have served from.

Detectives Swaby and Craig of Leeds C I D soon started a wide operation, with the assistance of the West Riding force. Bramley, being one of the satellite communities of Leeds cushioned between Leeds and Bradford, proves difficult to explore and contain. Too many transport routes cross there; the mill-workers who formed part of Annie's customers would not have been around at that time, as the mill had recently closed, so that cancelled out some local movements of people who might have been either involved, or have been witnesses to anything.

The woman's husband had died twelve years previously, and she lived alone in her three-storey house. The shop sold cigarettes, sweets and newspapers. A neighbour, Mrs Cook, commented that she did not know of any relatives of the deceased. So this quiet, lonely woman, very much like the case of Emily Pye in Halifax, was easy prey for a killer. She was a regular church-goer, attending the Church of St Peter in Bramley, where prayers were said for her.

Another factor increasing her vulnerability is the fact that the house lies in an isolated place, at the junction of Waterloo Road and Broad Lane, and a high wall, alleys and waste land opposite form a buffer between her road and a new housing estate. In other words, one has to conclude that the circumstances, material and human, were perfect for such an attack. The killer had every reason to be confident of success.

A similar case in Sheffield, that of Heather Hamilton, made the police consult with a mind to finding potential connections and similarities, but nothing came of this. The story proves to be one more instance in an ever-growing list of murders of lonely old women, such easy targets for ruthless people who are prepared to kill for money, but in this case, money appears not to be the motive. Stock and change were left untouched. The only other possibility is that, again like Emily Pye, there was perhaps a stash of money at least suspected to be there, and if so, it appears not to have been found: a needless, senseless killing in truth.

CHAPTER FIVE

The Killing of Henry Warner
1948

Today, as you turn from Leeds railway station, left into Wellington Street, you have a distant prospect of every possible symbol of 'the new Leeds': new businesses, building work in progress and a re-designed pedestrian-friendly part of the city. But in the dark days after the Second World War, there was something of a crime wave in the northern cities, and the robberies and attacks were mostly against businesses. Leafing through the newspapers from the year c.1946–1956, it is difficult to miss the number of attacks that nowadays would be called 'heists' in Hollywood crime movies.

The stretch of Wellington Street where Warner's shop was located. The author

But one unsolved murder of that time and in that street off Leeds station is far from glamorous. It was a savage attack on an old, defenceless man, protecting his own premises. He was beaten with a hard, blunt instrument at his shop early in March, and was still unconscious in hospital almost a week later, struggling for life. Before he died, police officers were sitting at his bedside, hoping for a recovery and some words that might lead to an arrest, or at least to a suspect. But he died without recovering consciousness and the inquest was held on 19 March.

Warner was seventy-seven-years-old, a portmanteau repairer, was found unconscious on the floor of his shop, with deep head wounds. He was found by two men around ten thirty in the morning, and had been seen alive an hour earlier

Hotel Metropole: just a few yards from Wellington Street, hinting at how this part of Leeds would be at the time. The author

by a Miss Battle, working at her kiosk. The coroner, Dr Swanton, stated that this had been 'a calculated and inhuman assault on an old and industrious citizen.'

Superintendent Bowman of Leeds C I D asked the public for help. Scotland Yard were involved; a photograph of the time shows four detectives hurriedly going down to the basement of the shop in Wellington Street, a sense of urgency in their movement.

The first momentous discovery was that of a large steel bar wrapped in brown paper. It was a packing-case opener and police were sure it had been used in the attack. There was also a lead concerning a woman wearing black, seen in the street during that time. The most promising lead, though, came from two passengers in a passing tram. At that time there was a large central bus station just a hundred yards down Wellington Street from Warner's shop and the trams were always busy too. A new blue-type tram, number 173, was the one the witness would have been on. Many buses and trams would have passed, constantly, and it comes as no surprise that one passenger saw something of interest; but she described the woman who had been sitting next to her, and on her right, with a view directly from the window. Police desperately wanted to contact the other passenger. All they knew was that two men were on the pavement outside the shop at about the right time, and they were loitering.

But the woman never came forward. Chief Constable Barpett wanted some help in what he called a 'gruesome' case. The most hopeful move seemed to be to trace the makers of the brown paper wrapping and a series of interviews with manufacturers took place. It was thought also that there might be a link with the Nichols, Bramley, killing of three years before, but it was not so.

Little chubby-faced Henry Warner, who wore pince-nez and looked like everyone's friendly grandfather, had been murdered and everyone was stumped. He had been based down in a cellar area, always a tough space to defend, and open to intruders. The Warner case is typical of that brand of murder taking place in a busy thoroughfare, and in working hours, when there ought to be plenty of witnesses, but nothing palpable emerges in the investigation. It was a bold, heartless robbery and murder, leaving an old man to die a long and painful death. The city of Leeds was suitably outraged, and people tried to help, but in the end, no witnesses were found and no leads established that might have proved successful.

CHAPTER SIX

Murder in a Rural Retreat: Ann Barker
Leeds 1948

Another elderly Leeds victim in the same year as Warner was Ann Eleanor Barker, aged sixty-five. But in this case the scene was not the busy centre of the city: it took place in the quiet country road called Ling Lane, Scarcroft. About three miles north of the ring road around Leeds, there is a scattering of beautiful villages such as Bardsey, Scarcroft and Cottingham. Now, they are for the wealthy, and provide a patch of the Leeds commuter belt between Harewood and Wetherby.

Ling Lane in 1948 was a very quiet place, and Ann Barker's cottage was then in an isolated spot. There is nothing left of the cottage today, though the place is still one of a long line of very spacious and attractive detached houses. As is the practice of many people in rural areas, Ann Barker kept a shotgun, and in her case it was rammed into a roofing area. But just after Christmas in 1948 an intruder (or just possibly a visitor) came into her home and battered her to death. No-one had touched the gun.

New housing developments on the place where the attack took place.
The author

Neighbours found her body lying on the floor near the door, and it is some indication of the closeness of the community at that time when it is noticed that friends came to see why routine had not been adhered to: her newspaper had not been taken in. She lived a quiet life; she did some cleaning for a wealthy neighbour, and had kept herself to herself, particularly after the death of her mother in 1945.

Scarcroft is an idyllic place, but the peace was disturbed once the investigation took off. West Riding detectives got to work doing house-to-house enquiries. One striking observation emerged from this which must have made the officers sanguine about some kind of lead. A man had been seen walking slowly down Ling Lane late at night. A witness noted that he was behaving as if he did not want to be seen, and had a 'slouching gait.' If he was the killer, he would have seen Ann Barker's lamplight and naturally, if he went to chase this up, he would have found himself in a place where he could take advantage. The search widened, and nothing more came of the sighting.

The far end of Ling Lane, between Leeds and Wetherby. The author

The work then switched to the one notable feature of the immediate vicinity that might have led to questions being asked: there was a hostel for Polish servicemen on nearby Wetherby Road. The primary material evidence needed was of course the inevitably blood-stained clothing that the killer would have. But the task of interviewing so many foreign workmen was gargantuan; interpreters were called in from Leeds University, but there were difficulties in the dynamics of the whole communication process. Most irritating for the detectives was the fact that, contrary to expectations, the Polish workmen had a lot of clothes, and had tended to throw away old clothes. It wasn't simply a case of looking at everyone's very minimal and functional basic wardrobe.

Fundamentally, what was the motive for the killing? Ann Barker was not wealthy. She had no hidden life, no secret habits or enemies. It has the hallmark of being an opportunist crime: the kind of assault a desperate stranger might commit thinking that the woman was wealthy and had cash around the

The Wetherby Road end of the lane, close to where the Poles were lodging. The author

house. One sure fact is that Ling Lane in 1948 would have been difficult to protect or to supervise. It is a very long road, quite wide. There is considerable space around all the dwellings, even today. If a silent killer did arrive and took her life for supposed gain, then it would have been a simple matter to do the deed. Noise would not have carried. It was winter and the night dark. Maybe the man slouching down the lane sensed easy prey.

One final pathetic detail is that the home where this terrible act happened was called Rose Cottage: just the kind of traditionally pastoral name one might give to a rural retreat. Now it is a name full of an awful irony. Even today, a walk along that restful road gives a sense of space and tranquillity: a passer-by would never dream of such an atrocity taking place there.

CHAPTER SEVEN

Hawksworth Mystery 1965

Senior Aircraftsman Robin Draper was a handsome man. His photograph shows a well-groomed, confident person, smiling, full of life. He had a lot to live for: a promising RAF career, a good supportive family, and a girlfriend. He had a passion for fast cars, and loved nothing more than to tinker around with motor engines.

But in a country lane in Hawksworth, north of Leeds, on 27 October 1965, his beautiful Jaguar car was empty, and Robin lay dead on the earth. He had been out to a party at the home of his girlfriend, Susan Marshall, a nineteen-year-old from Rowan Cottage, Mill Lane. He had left the party at eleven that night, and was found knifed.

The search began; police guarded and surrounded the scene and searched the outlying field by the light of arc lamps. Inspector Sam Cross was in charge and the search for the radio controller's killer was extended. The one real lead was the discovery of a woman's bicycle near the scene. Minute details were issued to the public, in the hope that a link would be found. It was a Hopper bicycle, with a twenty one inch frame and a trigger control on the right handle-bar. Police believed later that the bike had been stolen by a petty thief who had, for some reason, turned killer that night.

Draper was stationed at RAF Lindholme near Doncaster. His father was a maintenance engineer at Scalebor Hospital, and they lived in Burley-in-Wharfedale. He had known his girlfriend Susan since they

Robin Draper – from a contemporary sketch. Laura Carter

were at school together at Prince Henry's Grammar School, Otley. At one time he had owned four cars, and cars were central in his life, but on this occasion his beloved Jaguar was taken for forensic examination. No less a figure than the celebrated George Oldfield worked on the case, and headquarters were set up in a famous literary venue: the setting of the novel *Windyridge*, by W Riley. This had been a massive best-seller for decades. Fifty troops using mine-detectors joined the team.

The focus now switched to South Yorkshire. Police from Goole went out to RAF Lindholme to interview Draper's colleagues. Dozens of airmen were interviewed; police mainly wanted to know if any of them had been to the Hawksworth party. Nothing came of this plan.

The conclusion has to be that Draper, while being a popular man, and a skilled technician with a career ahead of him, either provoked some kind of confrontation – the kind that sometimes happens when automobile meets bicycle on a dark road, or that he was a marked man, perhaps in some love triangle? As with all unsolved cases, there are other parallel stories we need to know more about, notably more detail about Draper's life and relationships. But it is tempting to go along with the theory that this was the result of a heated and spontaneous argument. The only reservation in this respect is that there was no damage reported to the precious Jaguar that might have suggested an argument, or a fatal retaliation.

The latter line of thought also skips over any other possible motive. There was no robbery. No jealousy or resentment came to light. Enquiries into his professional life, many miles south and in a different social world, came to nothing.

The bicycle was apparently the best lead still. It belonged to a part-time worker at the nearby Fleece Hotel, and a sighting had been made of a man riding a woman's bike from Otley on the Monday night, the night of the crime. Eventually, an identikit image of a thin-faced man wearing a check flat cap was created. Six motorists responded to the call for help in following the bicycle clue. Once again, things reached an impasse.

We are left with a murder in a quiet country lane, within an hour after a party, and involving young people. It happened in a place well away from any crowd or public view. The more dramatic implication might suggest some kind of revenge. But surely the 'getting even' idea and the explosive confrontation are equally valid – and equally unproven. Many of the immediate circumstances suggest the possibility of some kind of altercation, maybe some macho bravado, and a tragic consequence.

CHAPTER EIGHT

A Shooting on the Bridge
1966

The whole area around Bridgend and the lower part of the Calls, just before a walker meets the main road towards Beeston and Hunslet, has a long history of crime and mystery. From the mid-Victorian period, the streets around the bridge have always been the home of drinking-houses, gin shops and various types of street crime, until recent times. A photograph of 1870 shows the cluster of shops around what later became the post office. At that time there was a bottle store, Henry Smith's beer-shop and Fernandes' very scruffy and run-down shop with lines of beer barrels outside.

For over a century, the thoroughfare had a particular geography which, as we can see with hindsight, offered very tempting opportunities for 'hit and run' or opportunist crime. In this instance, the place was 'cased' most likely, but there had been endless violence and drunken brawling in these streets for many years. The bus and tram routes to South Leeds were busy all day, and as Leeds sprawled new engineering industries around Beeston and Holbeck, the commuter traffic increased. In a district in which crime was seen as a 'business' armed robbery and assault were common.

But it was in much more recent times that Bridgend saw what was perhaps its most terrible crime, and the killer was never tracked down. What was many years earlier Hyams' clothiers, by a dark yard, was a post office by the 1960s. One day in June 1966, a person shot Mrs Winifred Sharp, working at the office. It was a heartless killing, done for a few pounds, that caused a furore across the country, as people became aware of the vulnerability of sub-postmistresses in particular. But the killer took more than cash – he took other items too, including postage stamps.

C L Lewis-Ford, President of the National Federation of Sub-Postmasters received a wide press coverage after this outrage. He pin-pointed the government's abolition of stamp licences as one of the causes of what was at that time becoming a daily occurrence – armed robbery. He said that 'hundreds of post-mistresses lived day and night in a continual state of fear.' He was talking about a growing market for stolen stamps, so there was more than simply the cash in the till as an inducement to attack.

It is obvious from the man's tone that the Leeds murder had been 'the last straw' and his indignation was directed at a legal system that seemed to concentrate on reforming the guilty rather than protecting the innocent. Leeds at the time, in common with other main Yorkshire cities, provided ample protection for those who were willing and able to attack in broad daylight, with knives or firearms. There was a warren of courts, ginnels and garths around that area. It had always been a place of dark corners and hiding-places. Being by the river, there were other routes of escape, along the bank, on foot.

The most likely explanation as to why the killer was never found is that he (and it seems from brief sightings that it was most likely a male killer) disappeared into what in London would have been called a 'rookery'. After all, throughout the 1950s and 60s most of the urban crime had been linked to business, to 'heists' and the newspapers of those decades can be relied on to provide plenty of gun crime. Even in the rural areas and very small towns, individuals were using guns. A common source for these was, naturally, service armaments kept by combatants when they were demobbed.

The few facts about the Bridgend shooting have the usual quality of frustration: the brief description of a man who was fairly likely to have been the killer is unhelpful: middle-sized, well-built, very short hair. Too many people passed by, and that usually means that no-one observes anything at all. Outside this was the normal concourse; inside it was late on and quieter. The assailant had clearly observed and picked the best time to strike. The routine appeals and searches, local enquiries, led to theories and speculation.

The plain but sad fact is that quiet, unassuming Winifred was yet another middled-aged and vulnerable person in a small shop, with no protection and her likely refusal to co-operate cost her her life.

CHAPTER NINE

Bingley Bookmaker Murder 1966

Fred Craven had just celebrated his sixtieth birthday, and he had been with friends at the Midlands Hotel to cut the cake, suitably in the shape of a race track. He was known as a happy man, 'a very friendly character known to practically everyone in town' as one local commented. But bookies tend to be targets for robbery, and in Fred Craven's case, he was attacked and beaten to death in his own shop, which was above an antique shop in Wellington Street, Bingley.

He was a very distinctive figure, as he was a hunchback; he was also known as part of a sporting family, and rather paradoxically, one contemporary report notes that he had been a talented sprinter when young. The spinal problem must have developed as he aged: whatever was the case, he was clearly not a sturdy man who would have been able to put up a struggle. But his family were well known in the area; his son played rugby for Bingley R U F C, and Fred had three daughters, two of them married.

Those were days in which bookies did most of their business by telephone, and running credit accounts. There are conflicting arguments about whether or not Craven was likely to have had money on the premises, but it seems likely. One account of him says that he would often carry as much as £100 on him – a

Bookmaker, Fred Craven – from a contemporary sketch. Laura Carter considerable sum in 1966. Yet other people state that he did not have this habit. But the only point that matters is to establish a motive, and robbery appears to be just that.

Amazingly, this is a case in which we know he died within a particular ten minute period, and we know that there were quite detailed descriptions around at the time of men seen outside his shop at the time of his death. His uncle Alfred, of Southlands Avenue, phoned to see if all was well at 11.20 that morning; just after ten minutes later he went down to the shop and there he found his nephew lying dead in a pool of blood. He had died from asphyxia, after inhaling blood, pouring from his fractured skull.

The notable feature of the murder is that it took place on a day when there was no racing in Britain, due to the weather. The last meeting to be abandoned, Sandown Park, was announced quite late. This is useful information, as it suggests that the killers were racing men and most likely local: punters know how quiet bookies' offices are when there is no racing. In those days, there would be nothing much going on – bets on the 'dogs' were rare as the meetings were usually in the evening. So there was likeable Fred possibly just catching up with office work, and the killers or killers arrived, working quickly and ruthlessly on taking both his cash and his life.

The men seen hanging around were sighted by many, and the descriptions are mainly that one had a dark jacket and

Bingley: a townscape from the 1950s. Laura Carter

cloth cap and was about twenty-years-old, only short: perhaps five feet five. The other was around fifty, wearing a trilby hat with the brim turned up at the back. The identikit was circulated widely, and £100 reward was offered by the family. Some observers had even seen one of the men leave a Morris Oxford, to walk to the shop. There must have been some quiet confidence that an arrest would be made.

The short time in which the murder happened is the most remarkable aspect of this story: he had phoned his uncle to tell him not to come, earlier that morning, and still within the ten to fifteen minutes already noted. Phyllis Kenny, who kept the antique shop below, had had a good view of the two loiterers. On top of the close sighting, it was also known that a very particular wallet had been stolen, and George Oldfield, leading the investigation, put out a description: it was plastic, brown, and imitation crocodile skin.

A house to house search and enquiries were begun; even more unusual was the nature of the business: punters working on credit often used pseudonyms. It was an age in which debts were run up and consequences were rather more marked and notable than today. Hence police appealed to the people who had their pseudonyms on Craven's lists: names such as Bricks, Dixie or Jay for instance. Pubs and cafes on the Bradford-Keighley Road were covered as well, and all possible moves were made to see everyone around the town who might have been close to the shop at the given time.

All was in vain. We have a case of a weak old man in a trade which has always provided targets for desperate men: a man attacked and killed in his own shop, and probably for not that much money. In 1966, we should recall, there were no defensive

grilles in betting shops; neither were there any staff in most cases, other than the owner. It was small-scale business, but it was everything to this kindly man. It was a handed-down business from his uncle. In every respect, this was the senseless killing of an amiable family man.

An artist's impression of the main suspect. Laura Carter

CHAPTER TEN

Murder by the Parish Church
Leeds 1968

Mary Judge was well known around the area of Leeds along Kirkgate, between the Parish Church and the Regent Hotel. It is a few streets of dark alleys, not far from The Calls – notoriously unsafe places for walks by night forty-years-ago. But Mary, forty years old and a cheery,

Leeds Parish Church. The author

The railway arches by the church. The author

sociable person, liked a drink and liked that area: in many ways a risky business, as may be seen even today, because there is a patch of land (now a small park and well maintained) under the railway arches. The trains above tend to swing around on the viaduct before going on into the station a short way further into the centre of the city.

Mary was discovered at just before midnight by a passer-by on 22 February, battered and mostly naked, with her clothes scattered around her body. She was only five feet five, with brown hair, and had been wearing quite garish clothes, definitely not colour-co-ordinated, so that would have made her noticeable. Her skirt was dark blue; the shoes green; white blouse, and her coat was a black check. She had severe head injuries.

The area was sealed off and arc-lights set up in that dismal, shadowy patch of land. Superintendent Hoban of Leeds C I D had barriers erected and asked about her life. She was well known to the barmen of the pubs around, such as the Brougham, the Regent, and other places up Kirkgate. People said she was 'always friendly and happy, liked a drink, and loved to stop and talk to children'. The patch of land is close to the Leeds central bus station, and at that time, the area was notorious for its attraction to beggars and tramps. Tramps would often cadge money along the bus station platforms. By day it was busy: there was a huge Pilkington's Glass office nearby, and commuter crowds would walk from the buses past the abattoir to Vicar Lane. By night, it has to be said, the area was well frequented by prostitutes too. Whether Mary was on the game is not clear, but one interesting point is that she lived in East End Park, on Glendale Street. This is along walk for her, up towards the Shaftesbury cinema along the York Road. If she was a familiar figure down by the buses, she needed a good reason to walk more than a mile down to the pubs she liked – and alone.

But Mary Judge's murder has a fascinating piece of drama to it: people saw her being attacked. This was because the Hull train rattled past the Parish Church at ten eighteen that night, and several people saw the assailant. A small boy was the main witness. He came forward with his mother and gave a description of a tall man of slim build, with long dark hair and wearing a dark suit. Of course, this was February in Yorkshire; but the train passed within a mere fifty yards of the patch of grass where the killing happened. The 8.37 from Hull would prove to be a key element in the investigation into this heartless slaughter.

Mary had also been seen outside the Regent Hotel in Kirkgate earlier that night, and it also became obvious that the killer would have had plenty of her blood on his clothes. Appeals were made to local dry-cleaners to be vigilant in inspecting clothes brought in for cleaning in the day after the killing. Nothing came of that, so the train sightings became the main lead.

The Hull train was so important that a reconstruction was staged. Officers boarded a train at Cross Gates, and P C Eileen Playforth took the part of poor Mary Judge. It took just fifteen seconds for the train to pass the scene; it was winter, late at night, and the grass was under the tall arches of the viaduct. But one positive thing emerged from this: a man was

Call Lane, a dangerous place at night in years gone by. The author

The piece of land where Mary Judge's body was found. The author

seen leaving the scene by a Bradford man, another passenger on that Hull train. At that point on the train's journey, and passing quite high above the patch of grass, the view would be quite distorted. But there was enough seen to make a helpful descriptive statement.

Yet all this work and methodical investigation brought no positive result. Mary, a friendly woman who may have simply been lonely, and not looking for men-friends at all, was brutally killed. But whether she was in the area for financial reasons or simply to meet friends, it had a certain degree of risk in that place at that time.

Part IV

Around Hull

CHAPTER ONE

Murder in a Dark Court
1854

In 1854, though it is hard to imagine it now, Dock Street and the half mile beyond, towards the Holderness Road, was a warren of streets going off streets, and these led to the dark courts: what in London might have been called a 'rookery'. These were good places to hide if

George Street, Hull, today. The author

you were on the wrong side of the law, but it must also be remembered that, as photographic evidence shows, they could be warm, family-centred places too. Images of these days often show two old armchairs placed outside on the asphalt, giving people normally cooped up some fresh air and conversation.

But it has to be said that this area, as for the stretch of East Hull beyond the old docks, the times were violent and trouble

A passage off Dock Street, showing how vulnerable walkers would be. The author

likely to break out at any time, mostly fuelled by drink and poverty. One case in this respect is that of Elizabeth Parker, a dock labourer's daughter of North Court, leading off Dock Street. Elizabeth was only fourteen when she was found dead in the water by young Thomas Hall as he mistook her body for old rags as he messed around in the shallow water.

How many times has the running of an errand to the corner shop led to trouble. Elizabeth was sent to buy some bacon and brawn for a Mrs Steele, who was a well-known customer at the shop, which allowed purchases 'on tick'. What happened was that Mrs Steel said she had never sent the girl for the goods, and her father stepped in. All this led to the young girl running off into the night. She was very upset, of course. This is the heart of the affair, and it turned out to be tragic. As time went by, concern for the girl grew and eventually, the police were called in. Now the tale becomes remarkable, if only for the lack of any real police work in investigation. This is because Elizabeth had told a group of her friends that she was running off to a moored ship bound for America, *The Pioneer*. Her friend, Lucy Forgate, who had been with Elizabeth in Lowgate, told the tale of the 'emigration' plan.

The lead was a true one, as Constable Hepworth went to the ship and was told that the girl had slept aboard on the previous night. Today, there would have been questions asked and in no uncertain terms, as the ship had left port not long before Elizabeth's body was found. The scenario seems so familiar it almost has a template in murder cases: a child sulking or afraid of repercussions, then he or she runs off into the night and into certain danger.

Amazingly, no follow-up regarding *The Pioneer* happened. The post-mortem examination showed that there had been sex, but (and this is a puzzle without more details) rape seemed unlikely. Dr King, in charge of this work, stated that she had died through suffocation, though there is no stress on definite violent or brutal treatment of her that might have led to her being strangled. The main fact about the condition of the body was that she was marked severely and in several places, with marks consistent with scrapes on gravel or nails. Much of this suggests that something very unpleasant had

The pool, view towards the eastern docks, Hull. The author

happened to her, and was not of natural causes. The verdict at
the inquest was 'found dead with marks of violence.'

There is an untold story here, that is sure. Everything points
to a murder here. The narrative is easily imagined: a young girl
arrives on a ship about to depart, and the last night before a
voyage without female company offers temptation to some of
the seedier and immoral characters living as seamen. Elizabeth
probably underwent a terrible ordeal in her last few hours of
life. What the whole case does enlighten, though, is the nature
of violent crime at that time and in that social context. Dozens
of similar crimes must have occurred in such a moral climate.

This is particularly important as a take on social history when we realise that policing the whole stretch of densely-inhabited land in East Hull was a challenge to any force, and that without advanced forensic knowledge, matters were tougher still. However, it still seems outrageous and amateurish in the extreme that nothing further was done to ascertain what happened on *The Pioneer* that night.

CHAPTER TWO

Wilful Murder at Cottingham
1901

The death of Anne Todd, a seventy-eight-year-old widow living in Cottingham, is one of the most intriguing cases coming under the heading 'unsolved'. This is largely because it has not been possible to ascertain any motive. The mystery is further complicated by the fact that her death took place almost a year after the attack, and clearly as a result of injuries inflicted on that day, 25 February 1901 when an unknown assailant or assailants came into her house by the back door.

Anne was found by a neighbour, Henry Ross, who had gone across to the old lady's house in Hallgate, Cottingham,

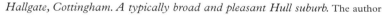

Hallgate, Cottingham. A typically broad and pleasant Hull suburb. The author

worried because the usual signs of her being up and about were not evident. After being urged to go and check things out by his wife, Ross went around to the back of the house and found that there had been a forced entry. Ann Todd must have been savagely attacked as there was a pool of blood on the kitchen floor. Her dentures were knocked out and were grotesquely placed in the blood. Her face had been severely beaten. The most impact was to follow, in that the house had been ransacked and furniture smashed.

But then, to Ross's amazement, the old lady breathed. Ross made her as comfortable as possible and ran for a doctor. After treatment by her own doctor, Anne was, rather surprisingly, looked after in her own home, rather than being taken to hospital. It seems staggering to note that she survived: she had been attacked with a poker, and her skull badly broken; the time of the attack was given as around ten on the previous evening.

At this point, any thoughts of this being a straightforward robbery and assault by someone preying on elderly residents in a wealthy, comfortable Hull suburb, the story steps up to

The street on Hallgate where the attack took place. The author

the level of high drama. Anne Todd, in the months following, was severely handicapped, and had only rare moments of any sensible articulate expression. On one of these occasions she spoke of the attack and said that the intruders were a man and a woman, and that the man had said, 'I'm going to do for you.' All Anne could recall saying is 'You'd better not ...'

Why was robbery not the motive? Because despite the destruction of the home, as if someone were searching for a stash of money, a purse with over £8 was found, and even some money wrapped in paper. If it was done for money, the only explanation could be that the murderers expected to find a very large sum hidden somewhere, and overlooked the amount of cash one would normally find in a purse, for everyday use at the corner shop.

Anne had been made into an invalid by this nasty, violent attack, and for almost a year she survived, obviously deeply injured by the brain damage, even though she was at times able to walk short distances. But she died within the year and a day specified by law for the definition of murder following an attack: in this case by person or persons unknown. She was staying with her brother-in-law in Anlaby Road when she died, on 1 February 1901. The *Hull Daily Mail* had no doubt that she had been attacked by more than one person, announcing an 'aged lady's strange visitors'.

One has to speculate if perhaps she had enemies in the area? Or we should ask who stood to gain by her death – and to gain what? If the murder was not done for purposes of stealing her savings, then it looks like the work of one or two lunatics, out to kill, maim and destroy property. There are instances of murder pacts, for course, as was the case across the Humber in the early 1980s, when two young men on a night out decided they should each kill a person. In Anne Todd's case, the words spoken by the killer seem to indicate a resolve, and with a reason: if the old lady recalled the right words spoken by the man, then he was there to kill and destroy – more in the manner of settling a score than in attacking for purposes of robbery.

The writer A A Clarke has pointed out that the local police had been publicly criticised not very long before this in the case of Mary Langley's murder, and inefficiency in this respect could be stated regarding the investigation into Elizabeth Parker, as in the last chapter. But we are left with those simple but resonant words, stated at the inquest held at the Newington Hotel on Anlaby Road: 'Wilful murder by person or persons unknown'. It must have been a sombre occasion, and it was several miles away from Cottingham: a very different area of Hull.

It should also be noted that Hallgate, Cottingham, where Anne Todd lived, is very much the same today as it was then, and a visitor notices how vulnerable a lonely victim would be here: a typical suburb with well-cared-for semi-detached homes, in a peaceful area, just a mile from the Cottingham hospital and the university. Though it has to be said that Hallgate is close to two quite busy thoroughfares. If the killers were in the habit of watching and choosing defenceless people in vulnerable situations, then they chose the right kind of terrain here. Several streets meet just a short way along from where the victim lived. But it is hard to see this as something committed by an opportunist killer.

CHAPTER THREE

West Parade Attack
David Ombler 1914

U nlike the murder of Anne Todd, this story of yet another elderly person attacked in their own home is patently one with a motive of robbery. But it has to be asked, how does a poker break? By the side of David Ombler, as he lay dying, lying in his own blood on 30 May 1914, lay a poker and some fire-tongs; the poker was snapped in two. If this happened in the struggle, then it can only mean that it was extremely violent, and that possibly the metal cracked on impact with a very hard surface – something much harder than the skull of an old man.

David was a market trader, and was always up and about in the early hours. Living in West Parade, he was in the habit of

Londesborough Road, where the victim lived. The author

walking to Humber Street market – a considerable walk, through town and beyond Prince's Quay. He was therefore reasonably fit, but he had had a long day on this fateful occasion.

When he was found on the floor it was clear that he had been attacked while eating breakfast; his food was still not eaten and he was still trying to melt some butter that was by the open fire. His cleaner, Mrs Harrison, found him. She came quite early in the day and saw some things out of place. She soon rushed out to find help, and local shopkeepers came in with her. He was still clinging onto life when the women came to tend to him. The drama escalated when first the police and then a doctor from Spring Bank came on the scene. There must have been a glimmer of hope that Ombler would survive, but he died in Hull Royal Infirmary a few hours later that morning. As Ombler was the brother of David, a councillor, the case had a certain degree of high priority. Superintendent Kilvington and a strong force of Hull C I D stepped into gear and a wide and intensive search began.

West Parade, Hull. The author

As with the Mary Judge case, there were several sightings and a few statements which clearly pointed to the killer being around the place, casing the house and planning the assault. Rumour and speculation ran through the whole city; but remarkably, two women in the street, Ethel Dibner and Hannah Feetham, had seen a strange male figure – he was leaving Ombler's home at around ten to eight, and he pulled his hat down over his face.

Police issued a close description of this man: the Chief Constable, George Morley, circulated a description stressing some quite marked features: mid-twenties, short, pale face and thin build; wearing a shabby overcoat and a dark cloth cap and muffler. The notice also listed some of the stolen items. There were many statements of mere suspicion, and the pursuit of these came to a dead end.

But there was even more drama to come when more people spoke up about that late night and early morning. A Mrs Robson told how late on the previous night as she went into her yard to fill a kettle, she saw a man jump off a wall neighbouring her property. Startled, she ran back inside, but she saw a man walking towards Spring Bank and there was dirt on the gate he had trodden on during his escape.

The old man had been robbed alright: items missing included a few pounds in cash, a silver medallion with a sovereign, and a silver watch. Timing regarding the killing was precise, as a Mr Moncaster had seen Ombler at seven thirty, just before going inside to eat. But even with the sightings of the likely killer being made by three people, and a good physical description, there was no arrest. So here was an aged greengrocer, living alone, killed by a stranger in a brutal way. His home was in a mess and there had been a fevered search for anything worth taking away.

The case is another within the Edwardian/Georgian years in which the Hull police failed to achieve any significant progress in a murder case involving old and vulnerable citizens. It was a story with a firm and noisy local presence: on one occasion police had tried to storm a house in West Parade, as there was a hint of a lead there, but the law of the crowd prevailed: the door would not be opened for them and there was uproar out in the street. There is more than a hint of desperation about this and such details about the *modus operandi* of the local force perhaps explains whey there was the usual call for Scotland Yard to come north, as they sometimes did if fresh minds and lines of thought were needed.

The verdict was murder by person or persons unknown yet again. Hull was a dangerous place to live in these years. The historian is surprised that no vigilante calls were given, nor, as sometimes happens in these cases, a scapegoat was found in the streets around West Parade.

CHAPTER FOUR

The Fish Shop Man
Samuel Smith 1930

Being a moneylender and handling credit for people is a high-risk business at most times; being such a man in the Anlaby Road of the inter-war years is surely a perilous occupation, and for an old man in particular, it would be something to make a good night's sleep a rare thing. For Samuel Smith, a grandad who appears to have found it difficult to live with others, it was part of the reason, one supposes, why he met a violent end in his own home on 3 November 1930. In fact, it was revealed after his death that the sum of £400 was owed to him by clients: a massive sum of money in 1930. Enemies hang around debts.

Part of Anlaby Road today. The author

His home was in Parkfield Drive, off the Anlaby Road, and at that time the whole street was only just built. The houses look all the same (even today) and most of the surrounding side streets are still unchanged, the only really contemporary feature of these few streets is the bingo hall at the end of the road. Sam was a former proprietor of a fish and chip shop not far away, but at the time of his death, he was handling credit and debt and had been sharing his house with daughter and son-in-law.

But people tended to move out of his way: he was maybe moody and difficult to please. The one photograph of him shows a man with a Lord Kitchener moustache, a strong, purposeful expression and a certain quality of sturdiness in his mien. But all this did him no good on that November day: he was beaten and choked to death, a shoe-lace found tight around his neck, and he had been battered on the head. It was a bloody scene that his son-in-law found when he borrowed a key and went in, to see Samuel sprawled out, lying in blood, with his pockets turned out. No problem in finding the motive then. Indeed that was the case. He had been robbed of a gold watch and a chain, as happened to Ombler earlier, and naturally, for a man dealing in cash some of the time, and apparently not using banks, some money would have been found and taken. An insightful remark was made by his grand-daughter, Molly – that he always found money to go racing. This would be mostly up the road at Beverley, one thinks, and of course, a betting man likes the local office too. For a quiet man, ostensibly retired since he became a widower, there are some hints of another side to his life: hints about possible sources of enmity.

It is easy to see a pattern in his story since that death of his beloved wife: turned in on himself, perhaps driving away his daughter (her husband, a sailor, found a job in Ireland), and then maybe getting into money problems of his own. We shall never know whether or not there was a motive of simple robbery – or a desperate attempt to retrieve some cash.

D S Howgate took control of the case, and Sam's last day was marked out as consisting of him being in the street in the early evening of the Saturday. A neighbour had said that she

Samuel Smith – from an earlier drawing.
Laura Carter

had seen a man leave Sam's house at a time in line with the probable attack. A large reward was offered: a poster proclaims a sum of £150. One or two details during the investigation would have seemed promising: the bootlace used to garotte the victim was mohair. That would have led to some fruitful enquiries one would have thought. Then a child found a wooden lat with a nail through it in a passage nearby.

Actions were taken by the killer that seem rash by any standards: he had washed his hands on a towel in the kitchen. He had also been so careless as to let the street see him: a Liz Parker had a very good view of a tall man leaving by the front door that

A View of Parkfield Drive. The author

Number 69, Smith's home. The author

night, going towards the back. Even more reckless was the finding of a felt hat belonging to Sam's son-in-law in a nearby side street. The hat had, naturally, been in one of the wardrobes. So topics such as finger prints, drawings and lists of stolen items were all available. The reward poster lists the stolen goods in minute detail: 'Gent's gold watch, keyless, white dial, English numerals' and so on.

Howgate must have been, if not sanguine, then at least hopeful, of a significant lead. One really interesting note is that the houses in this new street all had the same key (which is why the son-in-law had been able to go in), and the locked door (locked by the killer) as it had no sign of forcible entry, was therefore possibly opened by someone in the new street! It makes it easy to see that the killer would be known to Sam – possibly a client- and therefore let in without suspicion or resistance.

CHAPTER FIVE

Oswald Walker
1936

A photograph in the *Hull Daily Mail* shortly after the violent killing of Oswald Walker, a tool merchant whose business was in George Street, shows an old man with a grey head of hair, a severe expression, dark suit and neat, businesslike tie. His eyes are deep-set and his moustache well cared for. The figure we see is every inch the reliable, upright man of affairs.

The poster asks 'Did you see him last Thursday?' and the law officers were eagerly looking for anyone who had. The hard fact was that Walker had been murdered in his shop, and had been found by his worried wife and son. The son, Norman, lived in Hull, but his parents lived in Hornsea. It was a terrible sight that met them as they walked onto the premises. The old man, seventy years old but still working long hours, had been attacked and was covered in blood. They fetched a constable.

The body was found on a landing, and it became clear from the later post-mortem that he had been attacked from behind, partly strangled, and then bludgeoned, so his skull was fractured. The movement of the blood across the floor and into a ceiling suggested this type of attack. He was fully dressed, and the wounds were severe in the extreme.

Oswald Walker, from a contemporary sketch.
Laura Carter

Chief Constable Howden and Chief Superintendent Smith were in charge, and earlier unsolved cases of a similar nature were obviously in their thoughts as they set to work. It is notably significant, with the cases of Smith and Ombler in mind, that Scotland Yard were called in this time. Even the experts were presented with a puzzle. There were various aspects of the robbery which seemed contradictory. Of the two wallets the dead man usually had about him, one was still left on him. Also, silver and other valuables easily taken were still there. Maybe the killer had been disturbed? The crowds were gathering in George Street. The whole affair was big news.

Inspectors Sands and Griffin of the Yard were now in Hull. One of the first features of the place where the attack took place must have been the cluttered interior where cube sections of high shelves went up to a height of fifteen feet. Parts were ill-lit and an assailant could have successfully hidden, lying in wait. The obvious person to talk to first of all was the man's son, Norman, as the father had sacked the son

Dock Street. Now the location of the new Police H Q, but always a place for drinkers and trouble for the law. The author

earlier, due to Norman's more 'modern' ideas about strong-arm selling. But even more interesting was the fact that the boy had opened a shop in competition and that the last version of Walker's will left only a watch and chain to Norman, while his daughter had the important inheritance. These facts would have provided plenty of plot for the average thriller or murder mystery, and the cards must have been stacked against the son when this fact was known to the detectives. On the surface, it has all the ingredients for a family split with the potential for acrimony and hatred.

Norman must have been grilled. One can only assume that the long interview revealed aspects of his character that convince the officers of his innocence, and that there was no way he was capable of this crime. He had been well paid by his father - £7 a week was a large sum then for such work- and more importantly, the whole relationship has the hallmark of the father teaching the son some independence, rather than anything sour or rancorous between them.

Now came a key sighting: this was by a bus driver, Mr Lorrimar, who saw a man by the shop both on his journey into the city and on his return: so this had every sign of someone casing the property. Detectives agreed this attack was planned and thought out meticulously, so this would fit with that reasoning. The description of the man was not brilliant, but it made sense when placed alongside a story told by an assistant in the shop of a man who came in and talked with Walker by the main tool bench, saying he would see Walker again before he left. This man was in his thirties and had a scowl on his face. These two reports made the man the clear prime suspect then.

Time went on and nothing significant came of the regular police procedure. A conference was held, obviously a sort of 'think-tank' where all involved could brainstorm any possibility that came up for discussion. The central facts were that Walker knew the murderer, that a key normally kept inside was now missing, and that there was a basic physical description available. Other than this, nothing tangible was stated.

There was one major development a short time later, however: a lorry driver going by Doncaster had given a man a

Hull Royal Infirmary. The author

lift and dropped him off there at four in the morning. The telling detail here is that the man had handled a wallet matching the description of Walker's. This had been taken along with a whole raft of materials, some valuable and some not: banknotes, letters, a driving licence and photographs of his family – all sure to have been in a wallet matching the description of the one carried by the hitch-hiker.

Detectives Sand and Griffin were busy men. They travelled great distances to interview people with even the slightest connection or who might have had an inkling of a lead. To some this might seem a desperate move to simply look busy, rather than work related to definite clues. But it was to bring out the most interesting aspect of this story. This came in the shape of a man called Burson. The detectives came across him in prison in Birmingham and his tale was that he was a drifter and a chancer, and he had been twice to Walker's shop. But as with the Swaine case in Otley, the truth is surely that Burson was what might be called a fantasist. He made one statement and gave a long and complicated narrative of going to the shop in George Street, and after being found robbing, attacked the old man. But the officers must have been most suspicious when he then wept and demolished the tale: after all, much of the information could have been gleaned from the daily papers. However, Burson was interviewed yet again, after being tried for another robbery. Evidence indicates that it was his talk of working with an accomplice that kept C I Sands interested in this jailbird who seemed to know every crook and heist in the land.

Burson was mentally unstable; he typifies that version of criminal who needs the limelight, the one who glamorises the criminal capers and likes to feel that he is important, taking up police time. It came to nothing, though the story makes interesting reading, particularly as some of his details were convincing on the first of the interviews.

Then came the inquest on 13 May 1936 and it is incredible that a long document from Scotland Yard was read out to the court. Over a thousand statements had been collected in the investigation, and yet we still have those familiar words spoken at the end of it all: murder by person or persons unknown.'

The writer A A Clarke has written what must be in many readers' mind as they consider these chapters on Hull: could these cases, Ombler, Smith and Walker, be the work of the same killer? Yes is the simple answer. All that may be added to Clarke's perceptive summing –up is that through modern eyes, there are so many features in common in these killings that a betting man would maybe give you short odds-on that the killer was a Hull man with a canny local knowledge, a skilful application of covert movements, and a certain boldness in that he tended to have been seen – and each sighting gives us a picture of a night-stalker, one who sensed the old and infirm as the least troublesome victims.

Part of the bus route from which the suspect was seen. The author

The scenarios of these cases all comprise built-up areas, indefensible property, easy cover and darkness. The attacks all have the stamp of a brutal, ruthless killer who preferred the attack from behind , strangling followed by a blow, or repeated blows, with a hard instrument. The only exception to this is in the case of the one who would logically have had most strength and would have resisted most- the more fit Ombler – a man who could walk long distances and still do hard physical work.

The other repeatedly interesting feature of the unsolved murders in these twenty years is the nature of the local police force. Historians would point to the social factors of a port like Hull that make for these types of crimes: Liverpool makes a useful companion. People come and go; traffic is heavy and frequent. The city generated noise, filth, confusion; foreigners were among the crowds, men with less restraint if a criminal opportunity promised quick and gratifying rewards. If escape was quick and easy, and anonymity speedily attained, then the work of the law as always going to be tough. The streets off Holderness Road and Hedon Road, and the square mile south from the end of Alfred Guelder Street would have been a warren, difficult to penetrate and offering a den to any character wanting to keep out of the public eye for a while.

What a simple task it would have been to overpower old Mr Walker and a dozen more like him, transparently open to attack and robbery. It all looks so understandable with hindsight, but that is a cruel perspective, tempting for us now, but with a wisdom not considered in the early years of the twentieth century.

CHAPTER SIX

The Man in the Red Morris Car
Hull 1979

G loria Bielby may or may not have been murdered, but she disappeared, and incredible speculations have followed, many of them as crazy as fiction. Some people even rang police to tell them that Gloria had appeared as an actress in *The Professionals*. Gloria, an attractive blonde, married but living a separate, independent life from her husband Bernard, disappeared after leaving home early one morning – the 7 February 1979 – taking a number of belongings with her. She had often left home for extended stays away before, so there was no cause for alarm. But there soon would be.

Gloria never contacted her parents, family or friends again after that, and all accounts agree that this was just not the way she did things. If she had left home to start a new life with one of her many male friends, then that is not how she would have gone about it. We have to suspect foul play.

She was a happy, outgoing woman who attracted men wherever she went. She had been working at Reckitt and Colman's, and that company helped to forward the police enquiry when relatives became most concerned about her: she had not contacted anyone several months after leaving. From that point on, the Bielby case is shrouded in mystery and rises to a level of high drama and incident.

Naturally, as in every good fictional investigation, the top police detective on the case interviews the husband and the closest, most well-known boyfriend. In this instance, the latter was Mike Walker, a salesman and rugby player she knew well. Gloria moved in rugby club circles (there was even a brief theory that a touring team of players from Munchen Gladbach might be involved in her disappearance, but that fell apart). The detective was the highly-regarded D S Bob Carmichael, and he has put it clearly on record that he is totally satisfied that neither Bernard Bielby nor Mike Walker had anything to do with Gloria's disappearance.

A mystery remains, then. But clues and statements about her movements are available in great numbers, some contradicting others; neighbours saw her loading cases into a red Ford Escort late in the morning of her disappearance, and this did at least tally with the figure who is perhaps the one that police were most anxious to track down – the man in the red Morris car. What emerges from enquiries at Reckitts was that several employees had seen Gloria being picked up by a man with a red Morris in the months of July and August, 1978. She was always collected an lunch time, and descriptions of the man tally, but bear no resemblance to Mike Walker. This is indeed the man who is the key to the affair.

When the neighbours saw Gloria packing and leaving, she was with a man, but he was certainly not Blackburn: the woman who saw the whole movements on the morning knew Blackburn well, and so could say with certainty that the mystery man was not him. The neighbours knew the stranger well by sight, if nothing else, and even came up with a nickname for him – calling him Dapper Dan.

Over the course of the following years, tantalising scraps of information came through, but all inconclusive. For instance, in 1980, a man gave a much more detailed account of a man Gloria had been seen kissing in the Prospect Centre. This description seems to have been Dapper Dan. Yet rumours and frenetic media accounts of odd stories followed. On one occasion people were sure a body had been buried close to them and it must be Gloria. But nothing was found. Then, the water courses in Holderness were searched by underwater officers, but to no avail. The stories escalated, even to someone who was sure she had been seen in Venezuela. A woman's body was actually discovered on the North York Moors during this period, and that was not Gloria; this was going to be a cold case, and with no body to ascertain murder or any other cause of death.

Gloria Bielby was a lively, life-loving woman who clearly relished the company of men and enjoyed spending money.

When she and her husband had separated, he had given her £3000 and she had bought a car that says a lot about her character – a Ford Capri. One of her closest friends, Mrs Clyne, told the local paper that Gloria was 'attractive enough to have been a model and great company... A real head-turner in a crowd.'

Now, twenty-five years later, the lamentable fact is that her story is simply another one of those cold cases which may or may not have been a murder case, but all common sense and investigative reasoning leads one to conclude that she has been killed. Everything about her suggests a woman who would have kept in touch with her friends and family, and never, ever conceivably have melted away into consciously-planned anonymity. The bottom line is that Gloria enjoyed spending money and enjoying a rich lifestyle – and she obviously wanted to do these things within sight of those she knew.

Part V

Afterword

Cold Case Blues and Almost Solved

There are other fascinating questions to be asked, questions above and beyond the straight recounting of the preceding murder cases. These stories concern deaths which have an air of mystery, some that would now be solved quite simply, and some that have a sense of high drama and leave a tantalising unknown factor. A clear example of the latter is the Saxton Grange case, in which groom and handyman Ernest Brown was hanged for the murder of Mrs Dorothy Morton near Tadcaster in 1933. As he was to be hanged, Brown said something that could have been a confession about anything else. His last words could have been 'ought to burn' or, more intriguingly, *Otterburn* – a place connected with the famous 1931 unsolved case of Evelyn Foster.

This is very similar to the last statement made by Leeds killer Louie Calvert in 1926, when,

A typical scene for attack, and where Winifred Sharp was shot.
The author

as she was waiting execution, she said that she had killed old Bill Frobisher, a Leeds man she had thrown into a canal. The result was an open verdict on that one. Why investigate further? But technically it was another unsolved finally sorted out.

The dilemma of the cold case is indeed a sad and negative one: new evidence is awaited; science goes on discovering new forensic techniques and hope lies eternal in the human breast. But history has some peculiar cases, notably ones in which the outcome could have been murder or possibly suicide. This final section looks at some Yorkshire cases decided by science and one still unresolved, either murder or suicide.

Queensbury 1888

This was the double death of two lovers, their bodies found drowned but in different places, and it remains mysterious whether or not the young man killed his sweetheart before taking his own life.

It all happened at Jug Head beyond Queensbury, and the focus is Ann Pickles' suicide note:

> *When you find me, read this to my mother. I told harry what you said and you heard about him but you did not like it and said it wasn't right. It caused him to say he would not go with me and this drove me mad But tell him to forgive me for what I have done for I couldn't help it. Harry you're the first that's ever gone with me and you shall be the last…*

Now, this would be relished by modern detection expertise. Ann, it transpires, was very poor with her words. She was reputedly seeing another man and Harry didn't like it. The girl was found drowned in a horse-trough and then the young man's corpse was found drowned in a reservoir near Black Dike Mills. Had it been a case of 'if I can't have you then no-one will'? Not quite so simple, when it is stated that Harry was about to be a father: the mother a young Thornton woman.

But the heart of the issue is Ann's sister's evidence that Ann could not write, and had to spell out letters for her brother to write down. Today, a forensic scientist would have lots of things to say about the physical and the verbal evidence. How simple now, when, if a body falls from a tower block, as was the case with a Leeds killing not long ago, the pathologist may swiftly determine whether there is evidence of internal bleeding. But back in 1888, things were so basic and knowledge so small in these matters. Think what we could do now with that all-important 'suicide note' found under a stone near poor Ann's bloated body.

Everything about the story has the stamp of something that was paradoxically quite 'simple' for the J P at the inquest, held at the King's Arms Inn. Simple because the woman who laid out Ann Pickles saw red marks across her body, yet these were never mentioned at the inquest.

Almost unsolved! Kenneth Barlow 1957

There are unsolved cases in Yorkshire which are quite straightforward attacks: Harry Graham found in his taxi, battered, in 1944, or Mrs Comins lying in her garage in Scarborough in 1943. These are so typical of scene, method of killing and motive. But what about the complex tales in which science has to sort it all out. This was so with the highly significant case of Kenneth Barlow in Bradford. He was a nurse, and so when it came to his story about using a hypodermic needle to treat a carbuncle, it looked like this confirmed medical knowledge would help to clear him of any malicious intent after his wife died in the bath.

This happened in May 1957. Barlow and his sick wife had been in bed, but she got up later and took a bath. As he went back to sleep, his story was, when he eventually went looking for her, she had fallen asleep in the bath and drowned. He claimed he had attempted to lift her out, but there were suspicions raised when it was noticed that his pyjamas were dry. But the first forensic work confirmed that there were no traces of poison. Although she was pregnant, and there could have been a link or explanation there with any event leading to death, nothing was confirmed.

But there had been recent injections: there were puncture marks on her body. The eventual discovery related to the very high sugar level found in the corpse: the case became the first in which insulin was registered as the deliberate cause of death. The medical experts realised that in a murder case of this nature, the liver would be flooded with sugar, and so therefore would all the circulating blood, as a last-gasp attempt to stave off cessation of physical and organic functions. Some experiments with mice made this a certain consequence of injection with insulin – and as Mrs Barlow had been injected in the left buttock, the same was done to the mice. A parallel function was noted: Barlow was under suspicion. The longstanding belief that insulin soon dispersed in the body was impossible to detect was now not something that a killer could rely on. The fact that a previous wife of Barlow's had also died in suspicious circumstances took on a new interest for police. He was charged with her murder and found guilty.

Skull found at Gomersal : 1962 Murder
A man walking his dog in 1988 came across a pile of bones, and this was in an area which, twenty six years before, had been the focus of a suspected murder of a child , three-year-old Stephen Jennings, who had disappeared from his Gomersal home. At the time, all fingers pointed at one person: his father William. But no body had been found and there was a report that he had probably been abducted .

Jennings had a record, and even more indicative of guilt, little Stephen had been treated for injuries before that date. The child had even been abandoned, and was found wandering, undernourished, around the town. It was a simple matter to do what has been done for centuries – blame the gypsies.

In 1965 Stephens and his wife were arrested for neglect, and their marriage did not last after this. It must have been a major shock for him, all those years later when he was living a new life in Wolverhampton, for the police to turn up on his doorstep and charge him with the murder of his son. The truth was extracted by forensic archaeology. The now basic details of clothes, teeth, particular known injuries, all pointed to the corpse (buried under stones after being put in a sack) being Stephen.

The killer could contain himself no longer, and he cracked; his nemesis had caught up with him. The child had several broken ribs, and had been savagely beaten to death.

We should have the killer: Gorse Hall 1909

In the annals of unsolved murders in Yorkshire, there is one singular case which has come to represent that category of crime in which the suspicion as to the murderer is strongly hinted at in the bare bones of the story itself. The killing of George Storrs, a wealthy builder living at Gorse Hall, not far from Stalybridge, and just within the White Rose county, is surely a template for the 'crime covered for family' category.

On 10 September 1909, in that quiet spot in the hills, a man broke into the Hall and he was carrying a gun. Storrs took him on, after hearing the noise caused by his entry, and the man fled. But it was a warning. Less than two months later an intruder was there again – maybe the same man, now more bold.

This time, the man was actually in the Storr's living room and pointed his gun. Storrs was a courageous man, and certainly a man desperate to protect his loved ones; he managed to grab the gun and run to call the alarm. But the attacker was determined to achieve something, and he came again with a knife: this time, in a deadly struggle, the householder was mortally wounded.

The facts of the case are such that there was a prime suspect: one Cornelius Howard, and he was picked out in an identity parade by Storr's wife. Everything should have been cleaned up and a charge given. But everything hinged on the dying Storr's last words. He had struggled to say just one word in reply to the question, could he identify the assailant? He answered 'no' and then died as his blood ebbed away. Howard was Storr's cousin, in fact, and there lies the issue.

When another man was charged, a man fond of using a knife on people, Mark Wilde, it must have seemed like some kind of closure. Yet, despite the information that Wilde had once stolen a gun from the Hall, he was acquitted.

With hindsight, it has to be said that Howard was the most likely killer. What was going on in the family? If we ask what possible factors might keep a man from identifying a man whom he knew well, then we have to say either protection for personal reasons, or fear of reprisals. Bearing in mind the tendency at that time and in that place to use knives and guns in disputes (see the Uttley killing just six years previously and nor far away) then the latter appears to be the most likely theory.

Body down a Mine 1948

No-one would envy the task of the unfortunate rescue-diver, who, in December 1948, had to go under water at the bottom of an old mine shaft, looking for body-parts. But he found them. On a dark winter day near Wakefield, he had been asked to find the dislocated head and limbs of an unknown old lady whose corpse had been seen in the water by an official.

After enquiries, it was found that the dead woman was seventy-five year old Emma Sheard. She had been missing for seven years. Everything was apparently resolved when her great niece, still living at the address from which Emma

A street off Holderness Road. Poor defensible space for residents. The author

disappeared, confessed to the murder. But at trial it was not found to be murder. A whack with a hand had led to the old lady cracking her head. Mrs Hallaghan, the great-niece, had been useful with her fists and on a short fuse. Her criminal proclivities expressed themselves in a number of ways, including manslaughter and forgery. All these habits caught up with her at the Leeds Assizes in 1949.

This bloody affair highlights the kind of disappearance or supposed killing, resolved only with the passage of time. Hallaghan must have been a formidable and bullying person to live with.

Two classic Cold Cases: Huddersfield and Hull

This survey ends with two stories that have come to represent the intricacies and confusions, as well as the continuing human suffering felt by those who remain after an unsolved case, and most prominently in affairs in which the killer was almost definitely local. This applies to these two Yorkshire killings: gentle old Dorothy Wood of Fartown, and little Christopher Laverack of Hull.

Dorothy Wood's story tells of a life of duty, dedication and goodness; the fact that it ended in a brutal murder, as she lay in bed, is tragic. She was ninety-four when she died, and the killer is still at large. Dorothy was born in 1901. She was a nurse for twenty-seven years. She had worked as a Queen's District Nurse in Canterbury, and was involved in the application of a child welfare policy in Huddersfield in the twenties. She had trained as a nurse in Halifax, at St Luke's Poor Law Infirmary. A photograph of her taken in her fifties shows a kind, gentle woman, reserved and lively: an image of a woman fulfilled by a life of public service.

Not only did her life end violently, smothered with a pillow by a burglar who probably had no idea she was in the room, but it ended among her own people – in the community she had served for so long. As Graham Thurgood has written, 'She ran clinics and school inspections, keeping a watchful eye on children from the tender age of fourteen days to the end of their school life.'

On her ninetieth birthday, a photograph shows her cutting a cake, with two friends nearby. Only a few years later she was found dead by friends in her flat, a woman who was now deaf and helpless. She had had to write everything down for her friends. It is in this context that aspects of her murder become interesting: the reason is that the case has become a landmark, in that a man was convicted on the basis of an ear-print found on a window.

Yet the man was innocent, and after four years in jail, he was released after a highly unusual investigative action involving the police 'planting' a man in the cell next to the supposed killer, as he was in prison for a different crime, and then using this anecdotal information in the prosecution. In court, then, not only had a Dutch specialist in ear-prints given evidence as to the fact that the man (Mark Dallagher) had an ear that matched the print, but that the accused had spoken of the crime in such a way that he had specific knowledge. It was a miscalculation on the part of the law. After all, DNA had not produced anything at the scene; it was needed to be sure that the accused was actually in Miss Wood's room, rather than his

A typical West Yorkshire road, street corners and ginnels. Almost designed to attract criminals? The author

having been listening outside! He may well have put his ear to the window, but never have entered the home.

When a second expert said there was 'a remote possibility' that the ear-prints could have been left by another person, the case crumbled. This was in 2002, the conviction quashed. A more recent method of forensic study of ear-prints had shown that they were not Dallagher's. The affair is indicative of what can go wrong when forensic evidence is adhered to much too resolutely and unquestioningly. An innocent man did a prison stretch as a result.

As for Dorothy Wood's killer: he is still at loose. Someone that night entered the old lady's flat, having no idea that she was deaf and never would have heard the sounds of a forced entry. It seems sure that the killing took place because she had seen the intruder. How easy it was to silence her: just a minute under that pillow, which was found next to her body.

In an issue of *The Police Review* for March 2004, John Dean reported on what must surely be the ultimate blueprint for the unsolved murder in which the local aspects are the most prominent, and which goes on attracting further reasoning and speculation. The article was published on the twentieth anniversary of the murder of nine-year-old Christopher Laverack, whose body was found in Beverley Beck in 1984. He had vanished from the home of his sister in east Hull on the Friday night that March. He was to be supervised by someone in the family while the man's wife went out to work.

The baby-sitter had popped out to buy some crisps for Christopher, and on his return to the house, the boy was gone. It wasn't until two days after that a man walking his dog came across a plastic bag in the canal. The boy's body was inside this, brutally beaten to death and sexually assaulted. The weapon and actual place of death were never ascertained. He was wrapped in carpet underlay, and that was a potential lead.

The case has been large-scale in Hull ever since. Even over twenty years after the killing, there is a dense record of actions taken and efforts to find new openings. In 1986, for instance, someone offered a reward of £100,000 for information leading to an arrest. The newspaper features on the case have been frequent, prolonged, and increasingly desperate in tone.

The interest here, other than the heart-breaking human one of those surviving of course, is in the effect on the police officers involved. As with so many of the crimes discussed earlier in this book, in which accounts of the police officers' responses and feelings are given scant attention by the press, the satellite stories around the central murder case, are often ignored.

In this story, for instance, D S Peter Morriss is looking again at the 'cold case' and in accounting for this revisiting of old ground, it has to be noted that geography plays a crucially important part: usually in creating obstacles to success. For instance, the long area where the Beverley beck is, in terms of the finding of the body, is radically different now. In observing any disruption or development, the local police have to be vigilant, and in this case, it was realised that dredging work might bring to light a television, as a television was stolen from the house on the same night that young Christopher disappeared.

D S Morriss's work encapsulates the nature of the cold case re-investigation. In one sense, any discussion will encourage fresh thinking, and can only be beneficial, but it is obvious that his attitude expresses that of law officers, and indeed crime writers, when he says in an interview that the crime 'will not be consigned to history.'

When a Murder is not a Murder: Hull 1956

There are many cases like this one of James Jordan, too. This was an appeal, made in July 1955, against the murder charge resulting from a death in May of that year. Jordan had stabbed a man, Walter Beaumont, in a Hull café on 4 May of that year. Beaumont died of these wounds a few days after the attack.

This is a case of death my natural causes – an oedema – not necessarily the knife attack. Accident, self-defence and provocation were all put forward in defence. The whole issue was what actually caused the wound. So for our present purposes, the point is that the cause of death was either going to be the knife, or the medical condition. The fresh evidence called made it certain that there was doubt as to the stab-wound being the fatal cause. The earlier trial had proceeded on the assumption that the knife did cause the wound.

Percy Street, where the airman struck. The author

The famous Dr Keith Simpson gave evidence, and it was established that two other causes of death were possible: one was an intestinal problem, and the other was the result of medical treatment given at the time.

Here then, we have a story in which a man was (technically) innocent of causing the death of Beaumont. It might not be an unsolved murder, but it is an unsolved death! The conviction was quashed.

Conclusions

The unsolved murders throughout Yorkshire recounted here, and others occurring in South and North Yorkshire, make it plain that there are patterns and structures to the criminal acts involved. The outstandingly common scenario is that of the vulnerable person living alone, either in an isolated area or in a cramped, highly-populated network of streets in which violent crime is made easier to carry out. Typical examples, almost templates, would be the old person keeping a shop or living a more 'open' life in the streets, such as Mary Judge in Leeds or Sam Smith in Hull.

The number of murders effected in corner shops, and at times suggesting that the places have been well cased and the 'homework' done are very common indeed. Of thirty cases listed in the *Yorkshire Post* archive for c.1900 to 1970, twelve took place in shops or similar places of business, and a further four in the home.

Unsolved is a word that also covers a whole raft of crimes under the general heading of 'poison' and this of course, as with the case of the Oakwell overseer, John Sagar, and his wife and children (1854) exemplifies the issues here. Katherine Watson's book, *Poisoned Lives* (see bibliography) has shown just how common the act of the poisoner was in the Victorian period, and she makes particular mention of several Yorkshire cases, many of indefinite and puzzling outcome. She points out that at that time juries really demanded no actual medical evidence, and tended to convict people on circumstantial evidence alone. Surprisingly, however, the first case of evidence regarding poisoning presented in a court goes back to 1752.

The northern city protects the criminal: a dark court in Leeds, off Briggate. The author

In Yorkshire, in 1840, as Watson points out, people could buy an ounce of arsenic for two pence. How many indeterminate cases must there have been, such as the Rotherham instance of the death of Mahala Learoyd (1866), poisoned, as was realised after some time, because a little girl, Emma, had misread the writing indicating the amount to be dispensed. The example serves to illustrate just how many unsolved cases will be there in the records, either actual murder cases, or various versions of accidents and errors.

Poisoning and Infanticide: Unsolved for ever
The doubts and uncertainties of poisoning may also be shown in the case of Alvera Newsome of Heckmondwike. In this instance, there was a suspicion of incest in the family of Newsome, probably involving himself and his daughter. He was suspected of having tried to solve his problem by doing away with the little four-year-old who may well have been the issue of the incestuous union. After the child had died at home with the family present and no doctor called in to attend, the coroner insisted on an autopsy being performed, and the celebrated surgeon Benjamin Sykes of Leeds was called in. He confirmed that the child had been poisoned. Later, on being pressed to say more, members of the Newsome family admitted the incest, but there was no definite proof that the father had administered the poison. This was in 1801, at a time when druggists were able to set up anywhere, with limited knowledge and unchecked credentials, so a poisoner could travel well away from home, buy the poison, and there would be no local druggist to say that poison had been bought and no names given to the law officers.

The same could be said of infanticide generally: murders took place and it was impossible to chase the culprits and investigate successfully. Well before the nineteenth century, it was something heinous going on for economic reasons, and it is difficult to open up case studies now. For instance, in some counties between the years 1620 and 1680, the number of women accused of infanticide was around ninety.

Concealment of a still birth had been made a hanging offence in 1610. The examples of poisoning and infanticide open up a whole area of unsolved cases that, while pinpointing a dark aspect of social history, will always be unsolved.

Finally, it has to be said that investigations go on. From time to time, like the 1959 reinvestigation of the Bill o'Marks case on Saddleworth, cases are looked at from new perspectives. A cold case may become 'hot' with any chance discovery or fresh evidence. Oral history and anecdotal statements will always be given, though not always readily. The present author, on re-writing the story of Emily Pye in Halifax, met two people who had known the old lady, and who gave some anecdotes, mostly of a trivial nature, but these offered contributions about the woman's personality, and that is the kind of information often missing from enquiries at the time.

The abiding image in many of these cases, even those of a hundred years ago, is that of a suspect, described generally or vaguely, seen in a specific place, and never traced. The geography is usually a vital part of this image: as with the murder of Sam Smith, on a long street with several passages or ginnels running off the main thoroughfare. In the course of the research for this book, a story was told of a man living in the Quarry Hill Flats in central Leeds, in the 1950s. He was well known to the city police, and his killer was never found. It may have been a gangland vendetta. But those flats have long gone, obliterated to make way for what is now the West Yorkshire Playhouse.

Other oral history states that, in Leeds in particular, people disappeared along canal tow-paths in Leeds. The same could be said for most West Riding industrial towns. As we discovered when the Yorkshire Ripper started his regime in the Leeds-Bradford conurbation, the streets of these textile towns are abundant in suitable hideaways for people in trouble with the law.

The attacks recounted here have been mostly violent, brutal and ruthless: the words 'died without recovering consciousness' are forever at the end of the newspaper reports. What is rarely stated is the after-effects on a community. Stories of unsolved murders are also narratives of communities, and they offer a particular insight into the workings of these social groups. Often, the peculiarly working class culture of the criminal groups explains the varying codes of morality, such as the case of the Bradford mumming group who, in 1860, forced their way into homes to demand money for the performance, or the singular problems presented to the police in these rough northern towns when the populace were often a tough and hard-knuckled breed. In 1836, for instance, in Hull, a certain Jane Smith was charged with assaulting two policeman, the report was that she was 'of Amazonian build... she was handcuffed and her legs strapped.. it took five men to convey her in a cart to the station house.'

All in all, the Yorkshire context of these crimes, though, has the hallmark of the outraged community, as an attack on one of their own was the outrage. Richard Hoggart has described the mentality of Yorkshire communities as close in the sense that it might express itself in judging someone from a town only forty miles away as 'not one of us.'

Of all crimes, unsolved murders in such communities bring out some of the fundamentals of how people live together in these places; the outrage expressed in violent crime tends to highlight the foundations of the group morality.

It leaves the mind sour to think that the shadowy half-seen figure spotted by a murder scene may be the man next door or the reliable worker at the local factory. One of the first writers on nineteenth century crime, writing of a man called John Wilkinson, executed at York Castle, puts this well: 'Language affords no title by which we can hold up the assassin of a wife to execration.' Even worse, at the end, Wilkinson did not deny his crime.

The peculiar quality of the unsolved murder is that writers and commentators cannot even write about unconfessed acts. The killers are out there, somewhere. Whether it is a case of a massive dramatic scenario like the Moorcock Inn, with the wild Pennines as back drop, or whether it relates simply to someone like the gentle and sociable bookmaker Fred Craven, going about his daily business, *unsolved* is the cruellest adjective to use. We like stories to have a closure, and *closure* is the now official word used in terms of suffering and any emotional distress occasioned by the criminal act. The best hope of closure has to hinge on the understanding of and applications of DNA. As Russell Gould has said, 'Previous tests can identify DNA as belonging to one individual in fifty million; the new test (2002) increases the figure to one in one billion.'

If forensic science still has its limitations, then reading and reconsidering past unsolved cases has the other intrigue of the half-statement. There is no better example of this than the Saxton Grange case, in which before the noose was tied, Ernest Brown said the word 'Otterburn' (possibly) and thus invited everyone to look again at one of the most well documented unsolved murders of the twentieth century: that of Evelyn Foster, who was found lying on the grass close to her blazing car on the Otterburn road near Newcastle in 1931. The Saxton Grange killing was in 1934. Brown had burned out two cars in the process of killing his employer, Frederick Morton.

Most of the cases narrated above came from a world without the sophistication of DNA science. It therefore becomes clear that as social history, these histories provide a sidelight on grander social change and conflict. As most of these murders were for financial gain, it is not easy to sort out the social motivations: the intriguing cases are the ones with family ties and even more dramatic – family secrets. Secrets have a way of creating big trouble, and many of these stories show this at its very worst.

Not only do investigations go on: any death of a famous person will also attract wild theories if there is no definite closure, as in the case of the death of Charlotte Bronte. Simply because her husband, Arthur Bell Nichols, would not state openly that her pregnancy was the ultimate cause of her death. It seems certain that she had kidney failure and a poisoning of her body fluids that had nothing to do with any malpractice, though some writers have suggested otherwise.

Famous or unknown, the fact that a documented death has not been satisfactorily explained will always attract those who are interested in a good story – whether based on established fact or not.

Sources and Bibliography

Books and periodicals
Juliet Barker *The Brontes* Weidenfeld and Nicolson, 1994
David Bentley *The Sheffield Murders* 1865-1965 Alistair Lofthouse Design, 2003
Tim Binding *On Ilkley Moor* Picador, 2001
Norman Birkett (Editor) *The Newgate Calendar* Folio Society, 1951
James Bland *True Crime Diary Vol. 2* Warner Books, 1999
T R Fitzwalter Butler *The Criminal Appeal Reports* Vol. 39 Sweet and Maxwell, 1955
Marie Campbell *Curious Tales of Old West Yorkshire* Sigma, 1999
Marie Campbell *Strange World of the Brontes* Sigma, 2001
John Canning *Unsolved Murders and Mysteries* Time Warner, 1992
John Canning (ed.) *The Illustrated Mayhew's London* Weidenfeld and Nicholson, 1988
A A Clarke *Killers at Large* Arton Books, 1996
Patricia Cornwell *Portrait of a Killer: Jack the Ripper case closed* Time Warner, 2002
John Dean 'Cold Cases' in *Police Review* March 5 2004 pp. 22–23.
Mike Dixon *Ikley* Tempus, 2002
Charles Duff *A Handbook on Hanging* Journeyman Press, 1982
Clive Emsley *Crime and Society in England 1750-1900* Longman, 1996
David Goodman *Foul Deeds and Suspicious Deaths in Leeds* Wharncliffe Books, 2004
Russell Gould *Unsolved Murders* Virgin, 2002
Paul Langan *Valleys of Death* Breedon Books, 2001
John Markham *The Book of Hull* Barracuda Books, 1989
Robin Odell *The International Murderers' Who's Who* Headline, 1996
Louise Pearce (editor) *True Crime* and *Master Detective* magazines
Issy Shannon (ed.) *Milltown Memories* issues 1-7, 2002-2004
J A Sharpe *Crime in Eighteenth Century England* C U P, 1983

Sir Sydney Smith *Mostly Murder* Harrap, 1959

Donald Thomas *The Victorian Underworld* John Murray, 1998

Leman Thomas Rede *York Castle* J Saunders, 1829

Kate Taylor, *Foul Deeds and Suspicious Deaths in Wakefield* Wharncliffe, 2001

David Thornton *Leeds, The Story of a City* Fort Publishing, 2002

Graham Thurgood 'Dorothy Wood' in *Huddersfield* (ed. Nik Taylor) Tempus, 2000 pp. 27-33

J J Tobias *Crime and Industrial Society in the Nineteenth Century* Batsford, 1967

Harold Walker *This Little Town of Otley* R &S Educational services, 1995

Peter N Walker *Murders and Mysteries from the Yorkshire Dales* Hale, 1991

E R Watson *The Trial of Eugene Aram* William Hodge, 1913

Katherine Watson *Poisoned Lives: English Poisoners and their Victims* Hambledon and London, 2004

Newspaper archives:

Halifax Evening Courier

Courier Almanac

Huddersfield Examiner

Leeds Mercury

Lincolnshire Gazette

The Times

Yorkshire Post

Special thanks are due to the Longstaff Collection, for permission to use images from their photographic archive.

Index

PLACES